JUST WAIT UNTIL NEXT YEAR

By Carlton Welsh

MARTIAN PUBLISHING

Copyright 2016 by Martian Publishing Company

All rights reserved.
No portion of this volume may
be reproduced in any format
without the express written
permission of the copyright holder.

TABLE OF CONTENTS

PREFACE	4
INTRODUCTION	5
ZERO – Another Wonderful Football Season	8
ONE – Imagine: A Game with Action	11
TWO – Forget the Coach, Fire the Owner	17
THREE – Preaching to the Choir	34
FOUR – Yes, It's Personal	43
FIVE – Not Just the Refs Are Blind	54
SIX – A History of Misery	60
SEVEN – No Dodging This Draft	63
EIGHT – Prima Donnas	69
NINE – Coach 'em Up	75
TEN – Schemers and Dreamers	81
ELEVEN – The Commish	88
TWELVE – A Rose By Any Other Name…	97
THIRTEEN – Football Conspiracy Theory	100
FOURTEEN – Aliens In the NFL	104
FIFTEEN – Miracles and Mayhem	107
SIXTEEN – Setting Your Sights a Little Lower	125
APPENDIX	131

PREFACE

This book is a reflection of the stalwart fans of a beleaguered franchise.

The mantra that keeps us going is probably reflected in the fanships of many other teams as well. By the third or fourth week of every season, you can hear the mantra beginning. Usually, a whisper on the wind easily mistaken for the autumnal crying of the trees dropping their foliage. By week six, the whisper has risen to a buzz like the last annoying mosquitoes of the year and, by the middle of the season, it has become a veritable earthquake of grumbling fans having written off yet another season.

Hope springs eternal, even for the faintest of fans, those who can puff their chest out and proudly proclaim their affiliation and pride with the team colors.

"Yeah, we're having a run of hard luck now but… just wait until next year."

Yes… sigh… if only!

In these pages I knock a few players, the commissioner, a few owners, and much more than a few coaches, Like any other fan – both a seasoned arm-chair coach and Monday morning quarterback – my opinions are entirely my own and hold about as much weight as any other fan's opinion. Meaning, of course: not much.

Still, I hope it shows that, like most fans I had spoken to over the years, I have a passion for the game and the team(s) I root for. If my opinions are biased… what else is news?

INTRODUCTION

Football is a worldwide sport. Of course, here in America we call it soccer. And this book has absolutely nothing to do with **that** exciting contest. No, this book is all about what the world calls "American football" so *they* will not become confused. Here, we have no confusion; *football* is football and that *other game* is soccer.

The sport will be touched on a lot in this volume even though the emphasis herein is from the fan's viewpoint… the fan in this case being myself.

My complaints with the game are probably no different than fans of other sports franchises who do not reach the pinnacle. Let's face it: there are thirty-two football teams in the NFL and only *one* is going to win the Lombardi trophy at the end of the year. That means there are going to be a lot of anguished fans out there after that February Sunday. Of course, most of them will have gotten their Dear John letter a little earlier in the season, like even before the playoffs started.

In many ways, it is almost merciful that your team gets creamed during the regular season so the pain will end sooner. Following a team into the playoffs only to see them fall *before* the big game (or worse yet, **in** the big game) seems that much more painful. As the saying goes: the higher they fly the harder the fall.

Or something like that.

My current team is the Washington Redskins (or as more politically correctly known, I suppose, as the "Washington football franchise") and is entirely the result of geography. I live in Northern Virginia and it is the closest team to my home. Really close. They may play in Landover, Maryland, but their facility is in Loudoun county, where I reside, and I even run into the players occasionally. Yes, many of them live near me.

I have always tended to support the local team wherever I have lived and my support is a road map of my life: San Diego, Los Angeles, Dallas, Phoenix, Seattle, and Washington. Plenty of people carry their "home team" with them wherever they go but I don't do that. I enjoy the camaraderie and commiseration with other like-minded fans in whichever location I reside when the season starts. People here with affiliations to Miami and Jacksonville – for example – are pretty much all alone in their cheering sections.

Although I am not a fan of fantasy football, I know what that is all about. Dissatisfaction with the team put together by the local owner leads one to think that they could do a better job and that's their chance to prove it.

Others happen to like specific players around the league. I fall into that camp as well. But when these people come to face off with the Redskins, I root for my homeboys even though I can enjoy watching the other players.

Peyton Manning and Tom Brady are a joy to watch. I subscribe to the Game Rewind service at NFL.com (renamed GamePass just before the start of the 2015 season) so I can watch every game I want from the weekend just passed. All the games from 2009 onward are available and I have seen all the games in which those two played. (And, no, that is not a paid plug for that NFL service.) I keep asking the people at NFL if they are going to expand the archives to include other televised games going back to the NFL-AFL merger.

Funny, they never seem to respond.

Last season for the Redskins was all about looking forward to another monster season trying to figure out who they are and what the heck RG III is... Many said "Will the *real* Robert Griffin please stand up?" At least now that question has been finally answered: RG3 is a Cleveland Brown. And I am certainly glad that was cleared up before the season started. I mean it would look very bad form for RG to be wearing a Browns uniform when the Redskins took the field. (Was *that* random or what?)

Most the local fans I know are sitting on pins and needles, waiting, hoping, praying, that the Kirk Cousin destined for greatness – of which some glimpses were seen last year – will lead the team to another playoff berth. A lot of breaths are being held.

Much like the fans of the Pittsburgh Steelers did in all the years leading up to 1972 (they only posted <u>one winning season</u> from 1933-71) or the current fans of the Cardinals (the oldest football franchise and no championship since 1947), we are all waiting for that magic season.

This year might be your team's year.

The other thirty-one will have to wait. Again. Still.

I should also mention that this book is not an academic study of the game, this is about the game from the fans viewpoint and, as we are all aware, that view of the game can often be erroneous, misguided, or even dead wrong. I am probably one of the best examples of that.
Such is the life of a fan.

Carlton Welsh
the Ides of August, 2016

PART ZERO
ANOTHER WONDERFUL FOOTBALL SEASON

As I started with this volume, the 2015 season was four weeks gone.

Perhaps for most fans, it is a little early to start thinking about next season. But there are some teams – you know which ones – have fans staring at an 0 – 4 start and wondering what all the pre-season hype was all about; all that promise of the glory days ahead seem to have vanished faster than the morning fog on a summer's day.

Yes, those summer dreams have given way to autumn's sad fall.

Brady's Patriots – fresh off their victory over the demon overlords of the NFL – have kept pumping out the wins. Peyton, too, even under a new coach and a new system. The Bengals, Falcons, and Panthers are doing surprisingly well, as are the Cardinals and Packers. Perennial favorites, like the Ravens, Saints, Bears and Lions, have all stumbled out of the starting gate but I still cannot see their fans ready to give up the hopes for a resurrection during 2015.

The ones I am talking about are the followers of the teams who seem to find themselves fighting over the cellar every year: Buffalo Bills, Cleveland Browns, Oakland Raiders, St Louis Rams, Tampa Bay Buccaneers, Jacksonville Jaguars, Miami Dolphins, Tennessee Titans, Chicago Bears, New York Jets, and even the New York Giants.

A lot of people will complain about a few of these teams being cellar dwellers. Tampa has won a Super Bowl in this century; the Giants have even won two. But for all their fleeting success, New York has been kept out of the playoffs for the past four years.

Even the Redskins do not make this list because we have had one shining moment since 2011... sigh, yes, just the one.

Year of Last Playoff Appearance	
New York Giants	2011
Chicago Bears	2010
New York Jets	2010
Miami Dolphins	2008
Tennessee Titans	2008
Tampa Bay Buccaneers	2007
Jacksonville Jaguars	2007
St Louis Rams	2004
Cleveland Browns	2002
Oakland Raiders	2002
Buffalo Bills	1999

Still hopes are riding high for the coming season. Tebow fans were disappointed that Chip Kelly cut him from the Eagles roster just before the season began so it will be another year (apparently) without any religious controversy. And now that Deflategate has finally been put to rest, that rallying point for the Patriot-haters will have to wait for the next misstep by Belichick and his cronies.

All that's left for us now is to sit back and enjoy a season of football.

Keep a box of tissues handy. Though the miniscule distractions have been swept from the field, I am certain there will be plenty of erroneous calls by the officiating zebras to keep the bile flowing throughout the seventeen weeks leading up to the hallowed playoff season the fans are chomping at the bit to get to.

And there are bound to be a few injuries as well – and we all so fervently pray (keeping the Tebowing to a minimum, please) such disaster befalls the players of some team other than our own. Odds are it will afflict our players as well but we can at least hope the really bad stuff happens to the other guys… like the much-hated Patriots (except that Brady seems practically invincible) or the teams that really don't have much of a chance anyway, like the Browns – yes, even with Johnny Football in their pocket… or, well, he was there a minute ago… where has he disappeared to?

Regardless of the season's outcome, we will all find some shining moments for our team; touchdowns will be scored and some truly amazing plays will unfold before our very eyes to the wonder and dazzlement of the onlookers who will lament that such glorious effort was displayed in even a losing cause. We can all be proud of stellar accomplishments, brilliant achievements by the squads we admire.

And, as always, the glimmers of greatness can only fuel our belief that *maybe* next year will be the year these guys put it all together.

So, this book both begins and ends with that ever-hopeful vision dancing before our eyes in this – as well as any other – historic season where the reality falls short of the dream: just wait until next year!

Yeah, *then* you'll see…

PART ONE
IMAGINE: A GAME WITH ACTION

I grew up West Texas in the fifties and was an early fan of America's game – you remember, that sport that used to be number one before the Super Bowl stole the show? – and I would listen to the game on radio during the summer months.

There were no professional sports teams anywhere near where I lived. Having no local team to root for, I latched onto the one I heard about most often... you know, the one that won all the time: the New York Yankees. Yes, I collected the baseball cards and followed the exploits of Mickey Mantle with breathless anticipation.

Normally, I would hear the games on the radio but, every now and again, we would go to someone's house that had a television and get to actually watch a game. (Yes, back in those early days of television not everyone owned one of the things... strange as that might seem today.)

Being able to actually watch the game, it seemed a bit slower than it had seemed on the radio. At times, it seemed to draaaaaggggg. As a fan, I never really considered how much time was spent during the mind-games that took place on the field. The pitcher trying to toss a runner out after the guy led off from the base or waving off signals from the catcher. Hey, I'm talking really thrilling stuff here! When it was on radio, the announcer would keep a continuous string of talk going; on television you could actually see that nothing very much was actually happening.

Then, sometime in late 1958, I got to see a football game on television. It was quite by accident. I happened to see something really odd on one channel as I flipped through the stations. I turned back and watched for a time. These guys would circle up and the approach the other team, squat down and charge them. Mayhem ensued for a time before the guys would huddle up again.

And all that in the time it would take the pitcher to stare down a base-runner.

Forget baseball! Here was a game where something actually happened!

Maybe it was just me but it definitely did not seem to drag.

I was hooked.

Yes, even though, as the character Raj commented on the show *Big Bang Theory,* "Of course, it doesn't have the balls-to-the-wall action of cricket…" it was more exciting than other fare on TV like golf, bowling, or Friday Night Wrestling.

I reveled in the 1958 NFL Championship game, a match between the Baltimore Colts and the New York Giants that is still referred to as the "Greatest Game Ever Played". The game was a 23–17 overtime victory by the Colts.

Looking back, it was odd that I did not already know a little about football. After all, I was living in Odessa, Texas, land of the football-centric universe that was portrayed in Friday Night Lights. Permian High was to be my high school.

I was still a bit young at that time, but the next school year, I discovered they had school football teams starting in fifth grade. Naturally, I went out for the team.

I was the backup quarterback.

Playing the game was even more fun than watching it.

As time passed, I discovered my height was going to be an issue. Most the other guys were sprouting up like beanstalks while my "sprouting" was delayed.

Any dream I had for going professional in the sport was fading fast.

Texas Joins the League

Following the winners again, I would root for the Packers. That changed in 1960. We suddenly got two teams, if not precisely in our neck of the woods at least a damned sight closer than they had been. The Dallas Texans were rarely on television but the Dallas Cowboys – being the one of the pair within the ranks of the NFL – was shown on television most often.

And, boy, did they suck!

They and their fans entered the second season looking for their first win. After they moved past Eddie LeBaron, they were finally able to capture a few wins. Craig Morton and Don Meredith were both pretty good but it took the arrival of Roger Staubach to put the team in the championships.

After Staubach and Danny White, the team faltered a bit and I quit watching them as much. Not because I went over to being a Dallas hater (like so many have) but because I moved to Los Angeles, where there was actually a local team.

Moves to San Diego and Seattle found local teams there to support.

Eventually, I wound up in Phoenix and went back to following the Cowboys again until the Saint Louis team moved out west. Arizonans finally had someone local to cheer for.

Well, sort of.

The owner of the team, Bill Bidwell, seemed to do everything he could to ensure the team would never have a winning season. He changed coaches frequently (and chose poorly) and went out of his way to screw things up.

For example, it was the year the NFL put the two-point conversion into place. I remember it well because the Cardinals QB was the first to ever score an NFL two-point play. Tom Tupa was winning game after game after coming on to play after the starter went down. He won several games in a row and Bidwell ordered the fellow benched. Why? Because there was a clause in his contract that promised a tidy bonus if he won more than so many games.

When he reached that magic number, they benched him.

The season went straight down the toilet.

So, in a sense, I was already prepared for the world according to Dan Snyder. Bill Bidwell had been his opening act.

And things could, as I was to discover, just keep getting *better*!

Searching for That "Secret" Lane

I don't know if you're the type who invariably chooses the wrong line at a store, the bank, or the wrong lane in traffic. It seems whichever one I choose, it is the wrong one. I have learned to develop a great deal of patience and restraint from this happening so often.

Well, perhaps I misspoke about the actual degree of patience I have learned but I knew if I changed lanes then *that one* would become the slow one. Seinfeld spoke of drivers who keep switching lanes as if they were looking for the "secret lane", the one that was really moving.

I discovered this curse also works with football teams as well.

Moving into the Washington, D.C., area in the late nineties, I left the majority of my allegiance to the Cardinals sweltering somewhere in the sweltering – it's a *dry* heat – Arizona sun.

Now in the home of the Redskins, I figured my new local team would get to the playoffs a little bit sooner than it had seemed possible in Arizona. The Cardinals were retained in the Eastern Division of the NFL even after their move out west and so they played the Redskins twice a year, usually losing.

Yes, I had thought I had discovered that mythical secret lane.

Sadly, it was not to be.

Since I got here, Arizona has been to the playoffs a few times and even gotten to the Super Bowl, though they lost that game. And this year just passed, they were the first team with a guaranteed advance into the playoffs.

During that same period, Washington has floundered in the wastelands, slurping up the dregs in every year but one, which I will come to in due course. My plans of rooting for a winning team had vanished as fast as a desert mirage.

Passing – Torches and Legends

When I got here, the team had just completed their second season under Norv Turner, a very capable head coach hired by the late Jack Kent Cook. That late owner had moved the team from its digs in the

Nation's Capital at RFK Stadium and moved them to newer facilities in Landover, Maryland, which was to be called Jack Kent Cook Stadium after his passing.

Mister Cook did none of us any favors when he did not bequeath the team to his son, Cook, Junior, and opened it up to a bidding war. I suppose many people were okay with the idea and it could have turned out well, I suppose.

"Could have" being the operative words, of course.

Perhaps another owner would have been better for the club than Mr. Snyder but at least he was not as bad as Mr. Bidwell in Arizona. Snyder was at least willing to spend some money on his team. Sometimes a little too willingly.

For some reason, he had the impression you could just spend a lot of money on the really best players and forge a winning team. The idea is not new. In fact it was the basis of a lot of enmity in the early years of both the professional baseball league and the National Football League resulting in the concept of the draft and salary caps.

Owners having a boatload of money could not simply outspend the other owners or secretly smuggle in the really great college players. The playing field – so to speak – had been leveled.

Amazing Strides

A lot of the fans of the Redskins complain that the league ought to "do something" about Dan Snyder.

What exactly? He's an owner; he cannot be fired. And I have a sneaking suspicion that his presence helps a lot of the other owners… I am sure they can all sleep a little easier at night knowing *they are **not*** Dan Snyder.

But people carry this Snyder hatred a little too far. Just think of what amazing strides this fellow has had in only fifteen years of ownership:

When I moved here in 1997, I was told there was an estimated forty-year wait for season tickets. Today, there are season tickets to be had!

When Snyder bought the team, it was the most valuable sports franchise in the country, if not the world. Today, under his tutelage and with the application of his rare business acumen, it is now the sixth most valuable sports franchise in the United States! Not too shabby, huh? He's been able to move six positions in that short time. Today, both the Cowboys and the Patriots are worth more. By the time Snyder is finished, I should imagine even the Jaguars will be worth more. And that, my friends, would be some heady accomplishment.

    He has single-handedly created what amounts to a charitable enterprise. The entire club is almost a tax write-off (actually *ALL* NFL teams are untaxed). Quite a legacy to leave his children… Well, if he ever gets around to having any.

PART TWO
FORGET THE COACH, FIRE THE OWNER – NO, FIRE THEM BOTH!

When I mention the history of the Skins while I was here, I have to mention the one fact brought up by an announcer at every instance where we played the Chicago Bears. There has been bad blood between the two teams since 1940 when Washington met Chicago in the Championship Game that pitted the best team of the west against the best team in the East. Washington took a shellacking as the Bears romped all over them furnishing up with the most lopsided game in NFL history (not just any playoff game, ANY game!) by a score of 73-0.

It was before my time but it must have been a terrible game to watch… well, unless you were a Bears fan, I suppose.

Tedium on Tenterhooks

So many of the games in the period since I came to Washington are no more than a blur. There is so little on the plus side of the equation that the mediocrity seems to blur around the edges.

Most years started with high hopes and yet as many times the fan-base was not so optimistic. With the frequent change in the head coach position, it seems the team is having a "rebuilding year" every other year.

Much of that, I suppose, stems from the owner being impatient to win a championship. Real fans know that the championship is what you shoot for but, along the way, you put the very best effort on the field that you can. Most games should be winnable and the scoring should be close.

When neither is the case… Believe me, the fans know when something is rotten. The stench is palpable and all the spin doctors in the universe cannot cover it up. A team that plays poorly on the field is evidence of any of several problems: they haven't been coached properly, the game plan has been poorly managed, the coach has "lost" the locker-room, or – worst of all – the players don't care enough to put out their best efforts.

The first two items rest solely on the coaching staff. The latter two could be either a reaction to ineffective coaching, animosity among the players for one reason or another (usually because of friction between personalities), or pressure/interference from the owner.

As a fan, we rarely know what the real issue is with the team. It is a close family and there seems some unspoken code to keep the dirty laundry from public view. Getting the CIA documents released on the JFK assassination would probably be easier than cracking this nut.

The First Debacle

The first mess we encountered with Snyder's ownership came in the second season that he owned the team. In the first year, the Redskins had gone to the playoffs with a 10-6 record. They made it to the second round of the playoffs before losing to Tampa Bay.

The next season, the team was 7-6 with a pretty good shot at repeating the 10-6 of the year before with some "winnable" games rounding out the season. The previous two games against the Eagles and Giants had been very close nail-biters but victories nonetheless. The team was still looking good. Not great, mind you, but good.

Snyder proved to be very impatient and couldn't even wait until the end of the season to get rid of the Head Coach. Norv Turner was turned out with three games remaining to play. During the turmoil left in the wake of this move, it should not surprise anyone that we missed the playoffs.

From things I have read since that time, Snyder's disaffection with the coach preceded his ousting by several weeks. No, it was not a decision made in the heat of the moment. Perhaps that unrest was what led to the team losing four in a row before Norv got tossed.

Who knows?

Schottenheimer Nods Off – Spurrier Gets the Nod

Marty Schottenheimer was on a talk show on ESPN complaining about Dan Snyder. He was wondering how anyone could possibly work for the guy.

Naturally, Snyder offered him the job. And, quite naturally, Marty accepted the position. He had answered his own question about why someone would work for Snyder: the money, of course.

Marty improved on the previous year's 7-6 with a final standing of 8-8. It started out very slowly with five straight losses but things improved after that.

After a year, this arrangement was brought to an end.

Next, Snyder turned to the ranks of college coaches and brought in Steve Spurrier, a former Heisman winner and coach of the national champion Florida Gators.

In his first year, the team dropped from 8-8 to 7-9.

In the second year, they dropped to 5-11.

Then Spurrier quit and left.

The reasons for the disaffection have been rumored several different ways. Some think Snyder was disappointed at two successively bad seasons and forced him out while others say that Snyder went back on his word to Spurrier and was manipulating the players in some way. Whatever the reason, Spurrier was gone.

One thing that puzzled me about his short time as coach was the quarterback who arrived from Spurrier's first draft: Patrick Ramsey of Tulane.

For some reason, Patrick Ramsey had a hell of a time in Washington. Play after play, the defensive linemen would come crashing through and pummel Ramsey. I'm surprised he actually lived through it. The kid was tough, that's for certain. I heard later that more than once his wife was horrified to see how many bruises he had when he got home after a game. I'm sure she would have preferred if he had quit.

Ramsey had a degree in finance, so it's not like he needed a lengthy football career to launch him into broadcasting. His career goal was in another direction.

After noticing all the punishment he was receiving, I began to see a pattern with the collapse or holes in the offensive line: they usually came through Chris Samuel's spot. I found that hard to believe because Samuels was pretty darned good at his position and had been to the Pro Bowl several times.

Hm, I wondered, did Chris Samuels have a personal beef with Ramsey?

Even so, if such was the case, why didn't Coach Spurrier notice this fact? If it was so obvious to me, someone who just watched the game once, why didn't the coaches notice the problem when viewing the film over and over again?

After Gibbs came on the scene, we heard the rumor that Ramsey was asking to be traded. A couple of days later, both Ramsey and the organization denied the rumors.

Either way, Spurrier was gone at the end of his second season and I later learned that he disliked Ramsey and never wanted him as the starter. He wanted the kid he had coached in Florida: Heisman winner, Danny Wuerffel. So, I suppose he used the only muscles he could to get the kid off the starting roster: he planned to do a Greg-Williams on his own player.

Adding to the confusion, other articles I have read claim that Spurrier was happy to draft Ramsey but wanted to spend the guy's first year in preparing him for the big leagues. I don't know which story to believe but Ramsey getting pummeled repeatedly was a fact and how could Spurrier have *not* noticed it?

This reminds me so much of other coaches who tried to sabotage the personnel they were saddled with… Jeff Fisher, Rex Ryan, Jay Gruden.

Their vision of what the team needs is more important to them than people's health and well-being. How Greg-Williams of them, huh? And they certainly don't care about the fans!

Regardless of the workings behind the scenes far from the prying eyes of the fans, Spurrier was gone back to the college arena and Snyder was two years further along with a losing team.

The fans were getting restless.

Resurrecting the Glory

Hoping to bring a spark of life back to the team, Snyder was able to talk the legendary Redskins coach, Joe Gibbs into returning to the gridiron.

The fans perked up.

You could almost smell the championship on the breeze!

Or was that the smell of something else?

After all, if it didn't work, there were still some other retired Super Bowl winning coaches available, right?

Hold on, another one appears shortly…

2004 found the Skins improving over their previous 5-11 record. Yes they got a heady 6-10!! The good times were rolling.

Then, 2005 brought the pay-off: 10-6 and a trip to the playoffs. They beat Tampa (who had knocked them off the last trip to the playoffs) but then stumbled against the Seahawks.

The low point of Gibbs tenure was the death of Sean Taylor. It was a devastating turn of events that hit several people, like LaVar Arrington – the young man's first mentor on the team – extremely hard.

The next game was dedicated to Sean Taylor and the Redskins had it almost clinched as, in the final moments, Buffalo was trying a very long field goal.

Just as the guy kicked it, Coach Gibbs had called timeout to ice the kicker. The kick sailed wide.

They lined up to do it again and – for some insane reason – Gibbs called time out again. I know that maybe the pressure was getting to Joe and maybe the emotions of the tragedy with Sean was messing with his mind but even I knew you <u>cannot call successive time outs</u>. I thought everyone knew that.

As soon as he did, my heart sank. The kick had gone wide again.

They marched off the five yard penalty and re-tried the kick. Naturally, it was good and the Redskins lost the game.

Sorry, Sean.

Wrong Place, Wrong Time

After Gibbs' departure, the word was out that Snyder was looking to use the services of Mike Shanahan, the recently retired coach from Denver's recent golden days. Shanahan said he wanted to take a couple of years off and rest a bit before he considered getting back into another position.

Enter Jim Zorn. Former quarterback for Seattle Seahawks, he had been doing quarterback coaching for several different teams and had come to Washington to fill that open position with the team.

"Lucky" for him, Snyder needed a two-year head coach. Jim accepted the position.

It was to be a miserable two years for everyone concerned.

Snyder seemed to have simply put the team in a holding pattern for two seasons while he waited for the rebirth of Shanahan.

Zorn and the Skins went down in flames.

Toward the end of this two years lost in the wilderness, it was obvious even to the visiting broadcasters that Zorn was not calling any of the shots.

Snyder ticked off two years and contacted Shanahan again.

Zorn was shown the door.

Eureka!

Another Resurrection Attempt

This was around the time when I really started to get vocal about the dire situation with the team. Each year seemed to be a carbon copy of the previous regime and no one could seem to get a handle on what the problem was.

Well, other than a half a million fans.

The Shanahan era started with a boon. Philly was getting rid of Donovan McNabb and Washington picked him up. He was far better than anything we had seen in burgundy and gold for several years and had plenty of experience, especially in this division. He had taken the Eagles to the division championship many times and most of us thought he would do well here, especially when we played Philadelphia.

Things started well but then took a turn for Southern climes.

McNabb began to get erratic and – very unMcNabb-like – played horribly.

Like I mentioned before, us fans rarely get the real lowdown on what goes on in the trenches; both players and coaches have learned to keep their dirty laundry in the locker room rather than aired before the media. Most of them won't talk about the nitty-gritty even after several years away from the league.

So, most of the fans could not figure out what had happened to the great (or nearly so) Donovan McNabb.

Then we saw what the real problem was.

The "Shanahanigans" Era

We had suffered through two years of Coach Zorn (it's not that he was so awful, it's just that Snyder was filling the position until he could get *his* choice... and so never did much to support the two-year period of Zorn's position) to bring in the really great coach: Shanahan.

Funny, I thought he meant **Mike** Shanahan, but it turned out to be **Kyle** who's in charge. Oh, sure, they set it up to *look like* it was Mike who was in charge but it obviously wasn't so!

When McNabb was benched early in the season, Mike came out and gave his reasons... then back-pedaled and gave different reasons... then Kyle came out and gave different reasons and his Dad agreed.

At the end of the season, the Shanahanigans got even more obtuse. Mike was spinning his wheels, grasping for reasons until Kyle just came out and said that he did not like McNabb and was not going to use him!!

At least, Mike didn't have to come up with three conflicting answers this time but it became dreadfully obvious who is actually running the team.

Kyle worked with Grossman at Houston and wanted to put him in a prominent place in Washington. So, they worked Grossman out for the final few games of the season and I was thoroughly underwhelmed.

If Grossman had been using that as a display of his worth to the team, it was not a very good showing. He's streaky like Jeff George... and a few years ago we had a dynamite offense under Brad Johnson but Snyder wanted his dream QB: Jeff George. The Redskins tanked and Brad Johnson went to Tampa Bay and took them to a win in the Super Bowl.

And if Kyle is thinking this display puts him on the "fast track" to a head-coaching position, I think he's done a really good job...

That is, if any team is looking for a spoiled brat to run their team. If so, he's a perfect fit.

Hm, maybe if Jeff Fisher ever leaves Tennessee they can call Kyle and replace one spoiled brat with another.

Fisher did the same thing with Vince Young that Kyle did with McNabb: I don't like him and I'm not going to play with him! Yeah, that sounds *real* professional, huh? Why are they paying these guys so much money? To skate to the championships?

I hoped he would leave soon so Washington can find a real coach. (Which didn't happen, of course... this is Washington, fer chrissakes!)

And they talk about *players* being prima donnas...

That was the way the year ended. I can't say it was much different the next year except we had no McNabb to kick around anymore or blame for the offensive troubles. And Kyle's choice of savior, Grossman, was as streaky as ever. You don't get a final mark of 5-11 on the season with a decent QB.

But there IS light at the end of the tunnel. There are now younger players populating the squad and it would seem that Shanahan might actually be given the chance to grow a team. That is *Mike* Shanahan, not his son. I hoped perhaps Kyle and Grossman could go somewhere else the next year. Hopefully, the same place the unemployed Jeff Fisher wound up.

Regardless, Kyle saddled us with a quarterback of dubious worth and the season tanked.

Yeah, so what else is new, right?

We were almost bad enough to have a shot at getting Andrew Luck.

Almost.

The Savior from Baylor

Rather than Luck, we got Robert Griffin III. At once very personable, he started out slow but after the Bye week, he caught on fire. The team suddenly seemed unstoppable.

Watching RG3 play was almost magical and he seemed to play with the enthusiasm of a kid. Then Griffin got injured. The team seemed to implode.

Except that, once again, Shanahanigans came into play.

Finger-pointing, throwing everybody under the bus, and so forth, the team and the season self-destructed.

Yeah, we got to the playoffs but at what an awful cost.

The injured QB went in to play and re-injured his leg and made it even worse.

Neither the Redskins nor RG III was ever going to be the same again.

Trying to Buy a Championship

Unlike most seasons in the recent past, there were not a lot of undefeated teams past mid-season. It was such a strange season that even a team with a losing record actually **won** their division.

Since Daniel Snyder purchased the team, the playoff berths here have been pretty meager. Yes, we were not the lucky team who won their division with a losing record – though we did have a losing record. His desire to bring the team back to the glory days has been a little wide of the mark.

First off, he thinks you can buy a winning team. Several times now, he has shelled out the big bucks to bring in all the high ticket players to get on that fast track to a Super Bowl.

Ring-envy is not a pretty sight.

Needless to say, it has not worked out well. Having been involved in team sports when I was younger, I know firsthand that it is not just about the caliber or quality of the players that makes a winning team. It is not just having a great coach, either, as Snyder is learning as well (I hope).

It is a team sport and there is some very indefinable "something" that brings a group of people together and allows them to function as one.

The best football team in history (the undefeated Miami Dolphins) were not populated with the big-name players of football history. What they had, instead, was a great **team**. It is not something you can purchase or detect at the combine. The numbers crunched do not measure that potentiality. It is only something you can hope for.

One thing Mister Snyder could do that would help is to stop buying big name players (like Albert Haynesworth) and start valuing the lesser lights on the squad. Allow them to step up to the task. If the roster were peopled by players of that stripe, you could have a winning team.

Paying a few special players some phenomenally big bucks draws energy away from the TEAM.

The 2012 Outing

A lot of the fans here in "Redskins Nation" were disappointed and upset by the season-ending playoff game against the Seahawks.

I am not.

Normally, at least for most of the last decade, we Redskins fans would start looking forward with "maybe next year" around week eight or nine of the season, though some real pessimists (realists) started the mantra in week three. This year we witnessed a seven-game winning streak at season's end that gave our team the division and a playoff berth.

Yes, it is always disappointing when *your* team loses but, let's face it, only one team is going to play from here out without a defeat and they will be crowned Super Bowl Champions. Everybody else is going to go home a loser. No matter how good the team.

So, while the *way* the game turned out may have been a bit of a heartbreak, the fact that RG3 led the team into the playoffs at all is exceptional.

The only disappointment I had is that the football season – as in every other year – was drawing to a close, and I would have to wait eight months to see any more.

Oh, well.

At least it gave RG3 plenty of time to recuperate and prepare for the next "run to glory" as they play as the defending Divisional Champs.

The fans should relish that for the moment.

So, we could only just wait 'til next year...

Yeah, if only!

The End of Another Era

The next year showed us more sidestepping, people and players tossed under the bus and everyone blaming everyone else for not utilizing RG3 in a manner to get us back to the playoffs.

Straight answers were not forthcoming from any sector in the equation and another miserable season came to an excruciatingly painful climax.

Those of us who thought Griffin would be able to pull off the same magic as the previous season had not counted on the political machinations of the Shanahan twins.

Today, of course, Mike has been making the talk-show circuit ragging on RG3 for being the problem. He was so stubborn and unyielding that he would not take anyone's advice and threw away his chances.

Sorry, Mike, I saw what "throwing away chances" looks like (e.g. Johnny Manziel) but I could not see any of that in Robert's behaviors.

Shanahan has credibility because he helped get Elway and the Broncos to back-to-back Super Bowl wins. His cred should stop there. What he did – or didn't do – in Washington should show he has no credibility in the matter. He was **in charge** in Washington supposedly. He *should have done a better job* rather that acting like a bewildered sophomore caught in the headlights. (Mixed metaphors, I love 'em!)

Anyway, Snyder booted the father-and-son "I did nothing wrong" tag-team and went in search of yet another Head Coach.

He had hoped for someone of stature like the recently released Jon Gruden – another Super Bowl winning coach. Instead, he came away with Jon's brother, Jay. Another Redskin era was set to begin…

Actually, it just seemed to continue the broken system we had already seen.

How About That Real McCoy, Huh?

So, everyone was ragging on RG3 and expecting Colt McCoy to be "the guy".

One week he looked miserable against Indy but – after all – they were one of the premier teams in the NFL. With Andrew Luck at the helm, what would you expect?

But the next week? We were at home against the 5-7 Rams. Gruden seemed assured this was going to be a walk in the park.

Nope. More like a mugging.

People seem to forget that the reason Colt seemed so good is no one was expecting to defend against him and his technique of play. Once he was made the starter, we got to really see how ineffective he was.

So many of the fan sites I have seen go on and on about how bad RG3 is and how he can't make the adjustment to "pocket passer" like Gruden wants him to. Unfortunately, those people seem to know less about people in general and gifted athletes in particular, just like Jay Gruden. Like, nothing.

If I were Snyder, I wouldn't even let the coach finish out the season. By this point, his methods and his philosophy – not to mention his knowledge of football – have been proven to be sorely lacking.

And what was that about sending in RG3 with two minutes to go. Does he really think the star player really "needs to get a few reps"? I would burden Gruden with a few expletives but I try to keep this family-oriented book here and I will refrain from doing so, but feel free to blast him with whatever choice phrases you want. Please!

If the owner, Dan Snyder, understood football a little better he could probably make better decisions. Probably hearing Gruden's spiel about "pocket passers" are the future of the NFL... just look at Andrew Luck... he was convinced to go for it. RG3 is not a pocket passer. He is not a typical athlete. He is a gifted quarterback who plays the position naturally. It was not something he had to learn so Gruden is naturally wrong thinking he can merely "re-train" Robert. The kid was never trained to be a QB to start with, it's all just him.

Sure, he can learn schemes, formations, and so forth, but he cannot be untrained in the intuitive way he plays because it was never learned.

RG3 is truly a natural quarterback.

Fixing the wheel that isn't broken will never assist you along the journey.

But the Head Coach position is the wheel that's broken.

Anyway, how 'bout that Colt McCoy, huh?

Yeah, whatever.

Gruden Follies of 2014 Continued

I saw an interesting article at that time about RG3 and his supposed lousy mechanics.

You know, the game that Chris Cooley dissected to show how bad Robert was in his development.

Sean Hill, a quarterback's trainer and guru looked at the game film expecting to see a train wreck but came away with a different take. Not too surprising to me as it was what I got from watching the game as well. Griffin executed well and his fundamentals were in good shape – funny that Gruden (and Chris Cooley, among others) seems to have missed it, huh? But what would you expect from a novice – but what really bothered him was a porous offensive line.

Many say he should learn to trust the O-line but I think you first have to see something trustworthy. It reminded me so much of the beating Patrick Ramsey had gone through with his O-line – especially the supposedly great Chris Samuels – allowing him to get pummeled on every stinking play from scrimmage. No one in charge seemed to notice that little fiasco – but me, it seems – at the time so why should anyone there notice the parallel?

So, the fans were relieved to know that Griffin would be starting against New York in the upcoming game. People were relieved that Gruden has finally "got it right". But I was not so easily convinced.

Sure, Robert was starting the game but with Gruden's itchy finger, he could very easily pull him and thrown Cousins in. The problem, as I see it, is not that Griffin got the nod, it's that the game plan is still going to be Gruden all the way. And expecting the QB to suddenly become a pocket-passer without a suitable offensive line...

It just seemed a little offensive to me.

Perhaps if Robert had conspired with his teammates to play his sort of game instead of Gruden's...

But that ain't gonna happen is it?

No, these people are all professionals.

MockingJon

A nice article summed up the problem in Washington very nicely.

Jon Gruden was talking about the "mess in Washington" – and he wasn't talking about the dysfunctional Congress we have – but the Redskins football team.

Michael David Smith even hinted that the leaks from "inside sources" may even be from this same familial pipeline. Yes, Jay complains to brother Jon about his woes and seeks advice... Then somebody mentions it to the media... but I ain't sayin' who does this, of course... though his initials are probably JG.

Anyway, the tribe Grudenois is letting it be known that the problem with the Redskins is RG3 and that there is "no way" the Coach can work with the fellow.

We heard rumors that his mechanics were crappy... then QB guru Sean Hill went over the film and asks "where?"

We heard rumors that RG3 had "lost the locker room"... but those fellows don't seem to play any better for Kirk or Cort either.

It seems all these rumors coming out of Redskins Park support the claims of the illustrious novice Head Coach.

What a freakin' coincidence, huh?

Ain't he a marvel?

Okay, so I put this out there:

The rumors are from Head Coach Gruden himself to bolster his position against Snyder. "Ya see, Danny boy, everyone seems to agree with me."

And the one who has "lost the locker room" is Coach Gruden himself, otherwise the team would be a cohesive whole standing shoulder to shoulder with their coach, the game plans, the scheme, and so forth. Since all we see is a professional sports franchise in meltdown, I would say the problem starts at the top.

And this time, it doesn't seem to be emanating from Snyder.

This stench has JG written all over it.

One would also get the impression that the team would rather be doing something else, like getting behind the franchise QB and putting together a system – behind the superstar – and win some games.

Unfortunately, the players are professionals who know well enough to keep their opinions to themselves.

One can only wish that Jay knew as much, huh?

Party Like a Pirate

At the end of the year, it was all over but the getting down.

Sure, the Redskins had been a train wreck that year but the pitiful engineer of the debacle had received word that his job is secure for at least one more full-filled season.

Hot ziggity, huh?

RG3 made an appearance in the game on Sunday and looked impressive. With the exception of the TD just before half... and you know it was a robbery.

Then, in the second half, the spark that the old RG3 brought to the field in the first half was suddenly missing. He returned to dutifully standing in the pocket and getting pummeled.

The radio announcers – Sam Huff, Sonny Jurgensen, Larry Michaels, and even Chris Cooley were scratching their heads, trying to figure out what had gone so horribly wrong.

It seems rather obvious, doesn't it?

Robert came out playing like Robert plays and the coach got a bit miffed and told him to focus on being a good little pocket passer.

The results, of course, speak for themselves.

And next Sunday, Robert got the nod to start against Philly... well only because of Colt's injury, of course. It's not like he would start otherwise, huh?

So, we can watch and wait for Robert to be injured from the repeated punishment sure to come his way – Chip Kelly and his blitzers are salivating at the chance – and we can see Kirk Cousins coming in off the bench to assist this team to yet another wonderful 3 – 13 season.

Damn! I can hardly wait for next season when we can get to see more of the same!

Almost makes me want to be a swashbuckling Buccaneer. Like Brad Johnson...

Whoopee!

It's Not Like I Told You So...

That last season ended up in quarterback controversy but Gruden came out in early February 2015 to ease everyone's mind: RG3 is the starter. He said they were going to keep Cort and Kirk as backups but it was Robert's team.

This was reiterated – ad nauseum – all through the off-season and through training camp. It was the oft-repeated status quo during the start of the preseason.

Then came game two and everyone puzzled why that wunderkind, that future Hall-of-Fame Coach, that Einstein of football, Jay Gruden, would leave Robert in so long and with the second string O-line.

Most fans were aghast and horrified when RG3 got creamed and taken off the field.

Not me.

In the section just above, I outlined what Gruden had done to RG3 at the end of the previous season and – all his protestations aside – he got right back to where he had been at that time: trying to get RG3 out of the game.

Now Kirk has been named the starter and "unknown sources" within the organization are saying that the team is fine with Kirk as a starter… yada, yada, yada. Yeah, like what are they supposed to say, the truth? Not hardly!

They say what keeps them on the team and getting a paycheck. And especially keeps them out of dangerous situations on the field where the coach can maneuver *something* to end your career.

Most this stuff is so pathetically transparent.

Another Close Brush With Greatness

After months of proclaiming RG3 was going to be the starter, he wound up as the third stringer and did not play all year.

Kirk Cousins was the starter all year and set quite a few team records. They made the playoffs with a 9-7 record, then falling to Green Bay at home in the playoffs.

Gruden has got his go-to guy now and Snyder is probably feeling pretty good about their chances for the 2016 season.

RG3 was traded off to Cleveland to replace the errant Johnny Football.

I think that is probably enough about me and what I like about football. I could go on and on about the history of the game and all the really great stuff from the past but that is, as they say, history.

The seasons move forward and what's really important to most fans is the current status of their teams and the recent games.

Hey, that's why water coolers were invented, right?

PART THREE
PREACHING TO THE CHOIR

Yes, I have had few bones to pick about the way my favorite team has been managed over the past few seasons.

The Washington football team (Redskins, for the politically incorrect) is not the only team whose fans are hurting. And it has been that way since the dawn of time, since the first rugged cavemen decided to band together and defeat the cavemen in the adjacent valley. As long as it was just the two in the fight, their odds were fifty-fifty. The moment they added in the groups from all the surrounding valleys, the odds got worst and the wins fewer and farther between.

Rocket forward to today. The NFL is currently five years shy of their centennial. That's ninety-five glorious years of football under their belt. They have grown from a mish-mash of local teams in the Ohio League to the monolithic sports giant of today. There are over 500 football teams active today in a wide variety of local leagues around the world. The NFL currently has 32 teams but a phenomenal number of teams have joined in over the years to participate in the fun and die a quiet death.

Only thirty-two remain standing.

Of those, the oldest continuing football organization began in 1898, very quietly, as the Morgan Athletic Club. In 1899, Chris O'Brien moved them to the Normal Field on Racine Avenue where they became the Racine Normals. In 1901, he outfitted the team with used jerseys he had purchased from the University of Chicago, terming their faded burgundy color as "Cardinal Red".

From that, the club became known as the Racine Cardinals, joining the new league in 1920 as the Chicago Cardinals. The League would soon be renamed the National Football League. The Cardinals and the Decatur Staleys (renamed Chicago Staleys, then the Chicago Bears) are the only two founding members of the NFL to still be playing. The winningest team in the NFL (the Green Bay Packers and they *didn't* change their name) joined in the second year of the league, 1921. The Giants came along in 1925, Detroit in 1930, Eagles and Redskins in 1933, the Rams in 1937 and the Steelers in 1940.

Their fortunes varied greatly.

TEAM	Created	Years until Championship	Years since Championship
Akron Pros	1920	1	defunct
Arizona Cardinals	1920	4	68
Buffalo All-Americans	1920	2	defunct
Canton Bulldogs	1920	3	defunct
Chicago Bears	1920	2	32
Green Bay Packers	1921	9	5
Cleveland Bulldogs	1924	1	defunct
Frankford Yellow Jackets	1924	3	defunct
New York Giants	1925	3	4
Pottsville Maroons	1925	1	defunct
Providence Steam Roller	1925	4	defunct
Detroit Lions	1930	6	58
Philadelphia Eagles	1933	16	55
Washington Redskins	1933	5	24
St. Louis Rams	1937	9	16
Pittsburgh Steelers	1940	35	7
Cleveland Browns	1946	1	52
San Francisco 49ers	1946	36	21
Indianapolis Colts	1953	6	9
Buffalo Bills	1960	5	50
Dallas Cowboys	1960	12	20
Denver Broncos	1960	38	17
Kansas City Chiefs	1960	3	46
New England Patriots	1960	42	1
New York Jets	1960	6	47
Oakland Raiders	1960	8	32
San Diego Chargers	1960	4	52
Tennessee Titans	1960	1	54
Minnesota Vikings	1961	9	46
Atlanta Falcons	1966	n/a	n/a
Miami Dolphins	1966	7	42
New Orleans Saints	1967	43	6
Cincinnati Bengals	1968	n/a	n/a
Seattle Seahawks	1976	38	2
Tampa Bay Buccaneers	1976	27	13
Carolina Panthers	1995	n/a	n/a
Jacksonville Jaguars	1995	n/a	n/a
Baltimore Ravens	1997	4	3
Houston Texans	2003	n/a	n/a

A Short Look at Some Numbers

The Redskins won a championship after only five years in the league. That was a much shorter wait than the Packers; not to mention the Lions, Eagles, Steelers, 49ers, Colts, Cowboys, Broncos, Patriots, Jets, Raiders, Vikings, Dolphins, Saints, Seahawks, and Buccaneers, as well as the five teams yet to win a championship.

Many here complain about the last time the Redskins won a championship. It was all of 24 years ago. Looking at the chart above, we are still better off than the Cardinals, Bears, Lions, Eagles, Browns, Bills, Chiefs, Jets, Raiders, Chargers, Titans, Vikings, and Dolphins, as well as those five teams with no championship wins.

So, for all we have to complain about, we can thank our lucky stars that we are not in the same shoes as so many different teams.

And even these are luckier than some teams who never made it at all. How about the intrepid fans of Tonawanda Kardex? It was funded by the Kardex division of Remington Firearms' Rand company. They made business machines and later did quite well with something called UNIVAC. Today they are called UNISYS.

The Tonawanda team joined the league in 1921 after playing successfully against several teams in the league. They played only one NFL game. After being demolished by the Rochester Jeffersons to the tune of 45 – 0, they folded. Their fans were probably inconsolable at their disbanding.

Fortunately, they were better at business machines than football.

Long Time Coming

The Pittsburgh Steelers started in 1940 and were usually the worst team in the NFL year after year after year. Then came the NFL-AFL merger and they were offered a place in the AFC so the combined larger league would have an equal number of teams in both conference.

The Steelers said "Sure!" as they could not do worse than what they had been doing for three decades. Suddenly, they found themselves in a better situation. Drafting some great players helped, of course, but they became one of the more successful teams after the merger.

After waiting thirty-five years for their first championship, they have been in the Super Bowl eight times, more than any other team except Dallas and New England but have won more titles than the other two.

Another one that changed their fortunes was the San Francisco 49ers. They had been members of the All-American Football Conference begun in 1946 that had been completely dominated by the Cleveland Browns. When that league folded in 1950, two teams were absorbed into the NFL: the Browns and the 49ers.

Most NFL faithful claimed the upstart teams from the AAFC could not compete at the same level as the **real professional** league teams. (Does this remind anyone of what people were saying before Super Bowl III?)

Although they were right about the 49ers (they would not see a championship until Joe Montana came along) the Browns won the NFL Championship in 1950. They were in the championship game the first six years of their NFL existence, winning three times. And that was after being the AAFC champ in all five years of its existence.

So as much as the Skins fans want to bemoan their fate, there are other fan-bases who have more legitimate gripes.

Yeah, I know… So what?!

Curses and What-not

Before 1932's first championship game, the champion was decided by best winning percentage. The number of games played (which was different for each team) did not matter and tie games were ignored. Many of these games were played against inferior-quality (i.e. non-NFL) teams.

Some of the teams played as few as seven games (although one team only played one game) while others, with more aggressive managers, played as many as thirteen.

Early on, they had a rule about tie-breakers, to be used if two of the teams had the same winning percentage: the last game played between the two took precedence over any games played earlier in the season.

So, in 1921, the Buffalo All-Americans got edged out by George Halas' team even though their final match was supposed to be for exhibition, not for the standings. The Buffalo supporters named this the "Staley Swindle" and placed the curse on Chicago...

Funny, Halas' team went on to win several more championships and Buffalo, none. The curse seems to have been ineffective. (Unless it fell on the modern Buffalo Bills whose four consecutive Super Bowls losses are something of an amazement.)

The 1925 title was awarded to the Cardinals because the Pottsville Maroons had been suspended by the Commissioner, Joe Carr, just prior to their final "unauthorized" game of the season. The league gave the trophy to the Cardinals over the complaints of Pottsville.

Showing real sportsmanship, Chris O'Brien, owner of the Cardinals, refused to accept the championship when the league awarded it to him. He did not want a championship that way.

Later, when Charles Bidwell bought the Cardinals in 1933, he happily accepted the championship.

Now there is a supposed Pottsville curse on the Cardinals...

And I sort of believe in that one.

The Al Davis Curse

This one is not nearly as old as the others as it was born in the era of the AFL-NFL merger. The owner of the Oakland (the Los Angeles, then back to Oakland) Raiders was Al Davis, one time head of the AFL.

He was rather continuously at loggerheads with the league offices over many different issues. The move from Oakland and then back to Oakland being two of those issues.

His team's commitment to excellence saw them reach the Super Bowl on five occasions, winning the Lombardi trophy three times. This ranks them as the sixth best team in the NFL since the AFL-NFL merger.

But that's not a part of the curse. They win, certainly, but their players cannot seem to get into the Hall of Fame. I have heard many people mention this curse or retribution against Al Davis.

Jim Plunkett is the *only* quarterback to win <u>two</u> Super Bowls and not get the nod. Ray Guy, who practically invented what is important about the position of punter, had to battle long and hard to get inducted last year. The late Kenny Stabler, was not able to turn his Super Bowl win into a ticket to the Hall either.

Still, there are twenty-five members of the team inducted into the Hall. Considering that the other teams who were members of the original AFL fall much shorter in membership – Kansas City is the next highest ranking AFL squad at 17 inductees – I really don't think this curse is as bad as most people think.

It may have just been a PR move by Davis to win some sympathy.

And it may have worked.

Courting Disaster

I recently came across an article that had been written in October 2010 about the Redskins' Fan's Guide to the team and its owner, Dan Snyder.

The thing garnered a couple of hundred comments – none in support of Mr. Snyder, I might add – and died on the vine that is the fate of older internet articles.

Unfortunately for Mr. Snyder, he filed suit against the small paper in Feb. 2011 and the article was linked in the Washington Post online edition. Here it went nationwide and the number of comments grew to over a thousand.

People coast-to-coast got to read a little about what the Washington Redskins fans have had to put up with for over a decade now. He expanded his suit to include the author and the notice continued. After he finally dropped his suit in September 2011, the comments and views diminished greatly.

The article was referred to again in a recent Yahoo! Sports article and is getting commented on again.

People just "can't get enough of" or "have had too much of" Dan Snyder.

The benching of RGIII and the chatter about Mike Shanahan's imminent firing have kept the kettle on a low boil I guess. And then I heard that Kyle Shanahan, Mike's son and Offensive Coordinator, was threatening to leave.

Hey, Kyle, don't let the door hit your backside. I had been saying for three years that Kyle was the main problem the Redskins were having. I have even intimated that he was actually the one running the team.

Now an article from an "insider" at the organization, verifies the claim. Kyle had been allowed to surround himself with sycophants, buddies, and "yes-men" to the detriment of the organization. His bratty behavior did the team tremendous harm.

So Mike Shanahan is to blame for allowing his less-than-stellar son call the shots and eventually had to pay the price. So did Dan Snyder. So did all the fans.

Perhaps Mike was trying to "make a way" for his son in the NFL coaching world but I cannot think of an organization that would take him.

I am probably wrong on that score.
About Tebow being picked up by a team, I was wrong.
Perhaps I should say no "intelligent" team would hire Kyle.
That is, if there are any of those even in the NFL.

Show Me the Money

Continuing on the Snyder article mentioned above, people were complaining mostly about his avarice. Yes, he is bound and determined to make a bundle of money off his ownership.

So he sold the name of the stadium, raised ticket prices, and so forth.

The fans are complaining bitterly.

So what?

I moved to the DC Metro area from Phoenix where we had wanted a team for sooooo long.

We finally got Bill Bidwell to move the Cardinals from St. Louis to Arizona. Suddenly we had a team!!

Then, of course, he got rid of the really good players to save a bit of coin and raised the ticket prices. Yes, at one time the Arizona tickets were the most expensive in the league... and we did not even have a stadium! The team had to use the facilities at Sun Devil Stadium in Tempe which the ASU Sun Devils called home.

We had the same revolving door for coaches that currently plague the Redskins. We had the same "losing mentality" that Washington seems to have caught.

One year we had an exceptional quarterback that was actually winning games. But when Tom Tupa came too close to winning enough games to make his *bonus*, Bidwell had the fellow benched. For the season!

Of course the team tanked and they got rid of Tupa the next year and he will be remembered only for converting the very first two-point conversion in NFL history after that option was put into effect.

Buddy Ryan, the famed Defensive Coordinator of the Eagles, was brought in as head coach and he wanted to show everyone he meant **business** so he instructed the team to win *every single pre-season game*! And they did. Of course, the teams they played against weren't really trying to win...

Needless to say, the season went downhill from there, only winning three games of the sixteen that really counted. Buddy's legacy lives on, though, as his twin boys are in the NFL: Rob is the Defensive Coordinator for Oakland and Rex is the much-storied head coach of the New York Jets who has now moved on to Buffalo.

By the time I left Phoenix, people were as angry with Bidwell as the people here are toward Snyder. It seems all about the same to me. You gotta figure those guys are in business to make money and that's what they do.

Bidwell's son took over in Phoenix, I heard, and they got a stadium, got a decent team, and even went to the Super Bowl. That's great. Maybe that sort of thing will give the Redskins' fans some hope.

Everything today seems to be about the money.

The NFL jealously guards its "non-profit" status while they rake in the billions.

Facebook's Zuckerman keeps diluting his site with more and more ads. Google bought Youtube so they could stuff it with ads. Making money is the cornerstone of all these ventures in America.

How much is enough?

Maybe when every stockholder has bled the last stone dry...

PART FOUR
YES, IT'S PERSONAL

Since the start of this century, there have been two dominant players – although some may disagree with whether or not one or the other deserves such accolades – and most teams in the league have to prepare extra hard when they get ready to play these two: Brady and Peyton.

Between these two fellows, I think we could share out all the records that matter in the quarterbacking categories.

Peyton was supposed to be very good. He was drafted first in the first round in 1998 – exactly like the Colts got Luck several years later when they "moved on" from Peyton and Jim Irsay got yet another DUI.

Brady was not a prima donna, he was drafted in the sixth round in 2000. Most of the scouts saw this guy at the combine that ran like a duck waddling down the track. No, they didn't want anything to do with such a horrible prospect. So much for the metrics they use in picking the "great ones", huh? I think there are enough draft busts out there to answer that one.

Brady was 1 for 3 passing for 6 yards in his rookie season. The signs of his genius were still hiding under some bushel. But the next year, watch out.

In Peyton's rookie season, Manning passed for 3,739 yards with 26 touchdowns. Unfortunately, he also had a league high 28 interceptions. And, no, he didn't make the playoffs. He, too, was a bit slow out of the gate.

Since I do not avidly follow all the football news nor do I keep track of the coverage of the draft or which college player is which, the first I heard of Peyton Manning was in a commercial. Yeah, this goofy looking guy was tracking down workers in a grocery store asking them to autograph loaves of bread and such. He was such a huge fan!!

I had seen several such humorous ads with the same character in it before I even heard the name Peyton Manning. And it was probably a year or more before I put two and two together.

(Me = not sharpest tool in shed)

Hero Worship

Although my primary allegiance is to the local team, there are players I have seen over the years that I have followed regardless of where they were. Some came to my attention through other-than-football connections and others I followed because I saw them playing *against* a team I was rooting for.

In the 60's, I was visiting a classmate from school when his elder brother came home for a visit. He threw a few balls with us. The guy was Mike Curtis and I followed him and the Colts for a time after that.

Later a friend of my family was a QB for the 49ers. John Brodie was his name and I watched whenever I could.

Not all of my idolization came through familial connections. Sometimes I just saw a player than impressed me. One was a young QB who played with childlike exuberance: Brett Favre. Even later in his career, a touchdown was a chance to celebrate and he usually did with gusto.

The game was a lot different after his retirement. The first, the second, and the third.

I cannot remember having a grandfather playing the sport at any level before Favre.

I followed Eddie Royal through several different teams because he went to the elementary school where my wife teaches. He's come back and given gifts to the kids and visited with them. He does not live near the school – although I believe he still has family in the area – but I was impressed with his wanting to give back to the community he came from.

Having been a fan of the sport for close to sixty years, there are a lot more players I could mention but many of the names would be lost on current fans. A lot of the guys were quarterbacks because, as I said, I had been one on my school team, even if it was a short time.

Jim Plunkett and George Blanda were favorites as was Len Dawson and Jim Kelly. The last name I followed when he was in the only USFL game I ever saw. When he transitioned to the NFL, I had a reason to watch the Bills other than Thurman Thomas. (This was several years after O. J. left the team for a movie career and, well, other things.) And Kelly is the only QB ever to lead his team to four successive division titles and four *successive* Super Bowls. The sad fact is that he did not win a single Super Bowl but I doubt if we'll ever see that sort of dominance again. Neither Brady or Manning have done so... Yeah, I know, one of them may yet accomplish that feat.

There are far too many football teams, clubs, leagues, and players for me to try and go into all of them. While I was researching for this volume, I was overwhelmed at the interest in the game and its many variations.

Arena and indoor leagues are active in many cities all around the country and women even have a league of their own as well. Since they play their version wearing no more than bikinis, I am certain a lot of the male fans are hoping for "equipment failure" during some of the contact during the game.

Fans of football are like the fans of any other sport in that they want *their* team to win. By supporting the team, they get to share in the victories and wallow in the defeats. As Seinfeld observed on his show, "You didn't win. They *won*... and you *watched*."

Whether its baseball, golf, basketball, soccer, football, rugby, jai-alai, or any other sport, the fans hope and pray for a victory. Even if they only watch.

The Greatest Season

The Pats went undefeated in the 2007 season. Indy had a shot at the same but the management said they were interested in "more important" records.

Quickly, tell me who had the longest streak of at-home wins? Don't know? Okay, tell me who won the most games in the first decade of the twenty-first century? Stumped on that one as well, huh?

Well those were the "important records" Indy management settled for. Now tell me who was the undefeated team in football in the Super Bowl era... yeah, the 1972 Miami Dolphins... still, the *only* one.

Funny, but that seemed to me to be more important than those other two.

The other item the management felt would be the feather in their cap was keeping Peyton safe to win Super Bowl XLIV (44 for the Roman numerically handicapped). So, they kept Peyton safe but that Super Bowl was a loss.

Yeah, I know the Patriots rode their wave only to crash against the rocks of New York but that was 2007... this was 2009.

The team had gone 13 and 0 on the season with three games remaining. And the remainder of their schedule was what you would consider "soft". After they had pulled two touchdowns ahead, in the middle of the third quarter, the coach pulled the starting quarterback, deciding that the playoffs were more important than the remaining three games.

The coach would say that the owners had spoken with him and they decided the Super Bowl win was most important. As one of the bigwigs put it: Getting in the record books was the most important thing.

What in the world was that #&$%#&@ thinking?!?

Most fans could not tell you off the top of their head who won Super Bowl XVII or even Super Bowl XXXIII. But any fan could tell you who went completely undefeated ALL season to win the Super Bowl: the Miami Dolphins.

Zip! No one else. Bingo!

Now, what silly record book was this guy *thinking about*??

So, which was most important? One look at Peyton Manning's face as he stood on the sideline and watched his team lose the lead in the fourteenth game of the season told it all. I have never seen anyone more totally disgusted.

What should have happened at that point was that the coach should have woken up and put Manning back in.

I believe they would have gone 14-0, then 15-0, 16-0, and would have been riding so high that I think they could have coasted through the playoffs to win the Super Bowl. Seeing them go undefeated after the Giants had snuffed out New England's dream of that honor a couple of years before, would have been monumental.

And that would truly have been one for the record books.

As it was, they finished the season 14-2 and got creamed in the big game.

The owners and the coaches forgot the importance of momentum, inertia, passion.

And without passion, how can one player ever hope to elevate the game to something more?

The Colts, momentum spent, fell short of the big one, the really, really, BIG one.

Oh, but at least they had that consecutive home wins trophy huh? And that dazzling big marquee in the record books, right?

Lame-O.

In this season, when we have no Peyton Manning to watch, I wonder if that season ever comes to his mind. Hopefully not. The really great ones rarely look back with regrets. They remain focused on the future.

Leaving such minuscule conundrums to the fans who can only enjoy the glory through a more passive role. And dream of the Greatest Season that never happened but was once so close, so very much a possibility. But stolen by a group of suits that seem a little distant from what the game is really all about.

And I understand that too well because I am a Redskins fan.

With More than Just a Little... well, Luck

It seems that the NFL prophets (all 174 million of them) were right. Most people agreed since late September last season that Indianapolis, losing every game without Peyton Manning at the helm, was playing [i.e. losing] so they could win the Luck sweepstakes.

Sure enough, when the dust (and a lot of mud, slung as well) had settled at the end of the season, Indy had won the championship. They came out #1 in the Luck sweepstakes and proceeded to hint about dropping Mr. Manning.

After a few choice barbs exchanged via twitter and such, Mr. Irsay finally made the announcement that Peyton was no longer "their guy". In fact, such had already become obvious to most people since Irsay had already canned practically everyone else around the team's headquarters.

Funny, but I think the race to grab Peyton was even more interesting than Indy's sloppy season... well, watching grass grow – or die! – would have been more interesting than the games Indy "played" last season.

So, Indy cleared out a space for Luck... Peyton headed for Denver... Tebow moved to the Big Top in the Big Apple circus... and everyone just had to wait for the draft.

Then Robert Griffith III decided to forego his senior year at Baylor and enter the draft.

Hold the presses!!!

There were hints that Irsay was waffling... thinking about getting RG3 instead of Luck. Washington Redskins swapped some other draft choices to trade up to the #2 spot in the draft.

But which QB was Shanahan going to get? Luck or RG3? Things got pretty tense around many fans' watering holes debating he qualities of each of the young men in question.

I think they will both be good QB's but I always found Luck to be a little too serious. I guess that's okay if that's what you like.

RG3 always seemed more like a big kid, someone that really loves playing the game.

And smart?? Both of these guys rated higher in scholastics since practically anyone since Einstein played for the Princeton Potboilers back in... well, he never actually played, but I think he was drafted...

So, all the built up suspense was really nothing but smoke. Indy got Luck and Washington got RG3.

Great! but so what?

Can either of them field a decent team next season?

A quarterback doesn't make the whole team, you know...

Well, not unless you are Tom Brady, Tim Tebow, or Peyton Manning.

The nineteen are:

PLAYER	POSITION	YEARS	YR INDUCTED
Jim Otto	Center	1960-1974	1980
George Blanda	QB/K	1967-1975	1981
Willie Brown	CB	1967-1978	1984
Gene Upshaw	Guard	1967-1982	1987
Fred Biletnikoff	WR	1965-1978	1988
Art Shell	Tackle	1968-1982	1989
Ted Hendricks	LB	1975-1983	1990
Al Davis	Owner	1963-present	1992
Mike Haynes	CB	1983-1989	1997
Eric Dickerson	RB	1992	1999
Howie Long	DE	1981-1993	2000
Ronnie Lott	Safety	1991-1992	2000
Dave Casper	TE	1974-80, '84	2002
Marcus Allen	RB	1982-1992	2003
James Lofton	WR	1987-1988	2003
Bob Brown	OT	1971-1973	2004
John Madden	Head Coach	1969-1978	2006
Rod Woodson	Safety	2002-2003	2009
Jerry Rice	WR	2001-2004	2010

Did Hang Time Even Matter Before...

The Oakland Raiders are probably the least represented franchise in the Hall of Fame. Why? Well, Al Davis, of course. Al had so many run-ins with the league that they have pretty much ignored anything the Oakland/L.A./back-to-Oakland Raiders have done.

This was covered in the Al Davis Curse section earlier, as you'll recall.

But, yes, there are nineteen members of the black and silver who **are** in the hall of fame, according to the Raiders' own website. And one of them is that same Al Davis – but for some unknown reason the Raiders' site lists his tenure with the team as "1963-present"... Hey, didn't anyone tell them that ol' Al died a couple of years ago?

I am sure you will notice a lot of the names on that list did not have their most "hall of fame-worthy" years with the Raiders, they got their kudos in a different uniform.

Jim Plunkett is the **_only_** quarterback, I believe, to have won two super bowls who is eligible but NOT in the Hall of Fame, and he is never mentioned anymore. What a shame! That guy was simply incredible.

And there was an article about Ray Guy, their famous punter. See http://sports.yahoo.com/news/nfl--legendary-punter-ray-guy-frustrated--but-resigned-that-he-s-not-in-hall-of-fame.html

Those are not the only Raiders to be left out in the cold. Wide receiver Cliff Branch, quarterback the late Ken Stabler, center Dave Dalby, cornerback Lester Hayes, and safety Jack Tatum are just a few of the players who *should have been inducted years ago*.

But the reason these guys give for not inducting Ray Guy is that punters are not that important in the game. And with most the punters I've seen, I could heartily agree. But Ray Guy was different.

Dallas had, at that time, a punter who was also the backup quarterback, Danny White. The games with him punting were always exciting because you were never sure if he was going to kick the ball or pass it.

Guy was different, kicking was his thing, and he did it so well, the telecasters began timing his kicks. Never before had the concept of "hang-time" meant anything because no one else could kick the ball that high with any sort of control. And he was probably the best there ever was in pinning the opposing team backed up against their own end zone because his aim for the corner was pretty darned good.

So, yeah, punting is not that important to the game *most of the time* but when a team really needed a punter, they looked for the ones that were most like Ray Guy.

He became the template to measure punters by. And if that alone is not enough to get him in the Hall of Fame, I don't know what is.

I, for one, was never fully convinced that Troy Aikman should have been there either. His numbers were not that impressive and – more importantly – his team could win the really tough games without him. They did it without Michael Irvin too. But without Emmitt, they didn't stand a chance. But it was the strength of their

Super Wins that got them in the Hall. So why not some of these Raiders? It is time to stop the discrimination.

And if the guys on the voting for the inductees do not know football well enough to know how important Guy was, what the hell are their credentials for having a vote, anyway? Just because they have a fat behind to sit on doesn't quite seem like qualification enough... even if it is located on top of their shoulders.

I was happy to see that last year they DID finally induct Guy into the HOF.

Now, why are they not talking about Jim Plunkett?

A Seeming Obsession...

Many will, of course, noticed that I mention Tim Tebow quite a bit. I am a fan of both he and that other perennial favorite of fan anger – RG3 – and for the same reason: they both simply love to play. They remind me a lot of Favre in that respect: they just want to have fun and they smile and laugh a lot when playing.

Tebow did quite well in college and was drafted to go to Denver as a backup to Kyle Orton.

In the 2011 season, week 5, Coach John Fox benched Orton and sent Tebow in. The deficit was too much to overcome although he did score a couple of touchdowns.

After the bye week, week 7 found Tebow was their new starter. The game was in Miami – a usual jinx for the Denver team – and it was a record-breaker.

With the win, the Broncos earned their 400th win in franchise history, their first-ever win at Miami (in eight attempts), and became the *first team in NFL history* since the AFL–NFL merger to win a game after trailing by 15 or more points with less than three minutes remaining in the fourth quarter.

It was nothing short of miraculous. A lot of Tebowing followed, you bet.

More miraculous, they made the playoffs by winning the division.

Being the lowest seeded division, they got to play the highest-ranked wildcard. Mighty Pittsburgh was 12-4 for the season while Denver was only 8-8. Denver was supposed to be defeated quite easily according to the oddsmakers.

This game then became notable for being the first non-sudden death overtime game in NFL history with the new playoff overtime rules. However, the new rules only applied if the team that got the ball first did not score a touchdown, because if a touchdown or safety was scored at any time, the game would end. This meant that field goals could be kicked and *not end the game* for the first time ever. The Steelers lost the overtime coin toss, and the Broncos elected to receive. Shaun Suisham delivered a kick out of the back of the end zone for a touchback.

From the twenty yard-line, on their first play, Tebow fired the game-winning 80-yard touchdown pass to wide receiver Demaryius Thomas. It was not only the longest scoring play in NFL overtime playoff history, but Thomas also set a new Broncos' franchise record for receiving yards in a playoff game, with 204 yards.

With the win, the Broncos advanced to face the New England Patriots in the Divisional round.

Against Tom Brady, Denver would need much more than a simple miracle… and it was not to be. The Pats moved onward and the Broncos went home.

Next season, of course, Peyton came to Denver and Tebow was tossed out like last week's trash. John Elway, President of the Broncos, never liked Tebow. That opinion has been reflected by a vast number of football fans, writers, coaches, etc.

The reason I have always enjoyed Tebow is because he is different and he has the uncanny ability to win despite the odds, the critics, the metrics, or anything else.

Some religious fanatics attribute it to God being on his side or something. Even Joel Osteen had an interesting joke about it. Tom Brady had died and gone to heaven and God was showing him around. The house he got was nice and all but he noticed a much bigger and plusher pad decked out in orange and blue, with a swimming pool in the shape of Denver's bronco. Brady said, "I've won four Super Bowls. Why does Tebow get a bigger house than mine?" To which God replied, "That's not Tebow's house... that's mine."

I know many today are obsessed with numbers – statistics and numbers dominate discussions around the water coolers – and with science being so very important in our world today, the dependence on metrics is understandable. Having played in team sports for many years, I believe there is something more than simply the numbers that guide the human spirit in such endeavors.

Otherwise, what would be the point of even playing the game, huh? Match them up numerically and decide who the winner is and call it a day. Fortunately, there is something in us, especially during some competitive moments that transcend the numbers and blows away expectations.

Sure, Tebow does not look like the numbers you want but, let's face it, the guy has a certain something – a contagious enthusiasm if nothing else – that lifts those around him to accomplish more than what the doubters think.

And isn't that really at the heart of what being a fan is all about? Believing.

PART FIVE
NOT JUST THE REFS ARE BLIND

Here in the twenty-first century, science rules.

Around the NFL it has ruled for a bit longer and a lot of columnists, coaches and scouts have depended on developing a "system" that can be used adequately to predict the potential of any given player.

You might as well contact a soothsayer with a crystal ball.

For all the vaunted mathematics used over the years, there is a disproportionate number of "draft busts" to show that the system being used is in need of a little – more or less – tweaking.

Not only this sport, for certain, but there was a basketball player who came out of college a few years back and was drafted by the Phoenix Suns. Hopes were high that this guy would take them to the championship game.

The result? The guy was mediocre at best and never seem to give more than 50% during any of the games. Seems he played so well for four years in college *in order to* get a huge contract with a massive signing bonus. With that many millions, he would be set up for life even if he did nothing ever again.

It worked.

Phoenix traded him off and the next club where the young man got another sizeable chunk of change. A year later, he was gone from professional basketball.

Some people know how to use the "system" to their own ends.

This is not to imply that there are a lot of those people around. No, most guys get into professional sports in the hopes of making it their career… for *years*, not just for a bit of coin in their piggy banks.

Most of these players have the hearts built for competition.

Still, the busts should tell these people that something is wrong with their system.

The Numbers Work... But Not All the Time

Let's look at an example.

Peyton Manning came out of college with great numbers. Everyone knew he was going to be awesome in the NFL which, as everyone knows, he was. Not only did he lead the league in all sorts of stats (numbers again, huh?) but he got into the playoffs consistently, even getting to the Super Bowl a number of times.

He did it twice with the Colts – winning one time – and then twice with the Broncos – winning once there as well.

He was *supposed* to be that good.

When his younger brother, Eli, was coming into the league, Peyton told everyone, "If you think I'm good, wait 'til you see Eli."

It's great to have an older brother that supportive and even if Eli's numbers were not on par with Peyton's, he was able to win two Super Bowls first.

So, Peyton's career stands as the standard for using the metrics used by scouts.

Now, let's look at the other contender for "greatest" currently playing: Tom Brady.

This fellow came out sub-par out of college. Scouts who saw him at the combine noted he was sluggish in movement and his running "resembled the waddling of a duck". Other quarterbacks were taken ahead of him in the draft and he wasn't picked up until round six.

Sixth round!

Today he has as many Super Bowl rings as anyone else in history, and his career seems to be far from over.

So much for the metrics used, huh? How many saw that coming?

Other than perhaps Bill Belichick, probably no one.

Brady-Haters

Notwithstanding the victories posted by Tom Brady and the Patriots – or perhaps *because of* their dominance – many people dislike the New England team.

Certainly, Belichick pushes the envelope at times and has, at times, gone a little too far. He usually pays the fines and keeps moving along to another little experiment.

Many times I have heard people ragging on "yet another scandal" concerning the Patriots and Tom Brady with some sportswriters even saying it might tarnish Brady's chances for getting into the HOF.

Pleeeeze, don't be ridiculous. Brady will be inducted in his first year of eligibility. And all those Brady-bashers who smirked that he was "going down" because of deflategate haven't really got a clue.

People seem to hate Tom because he's the golden boy of football. They seem to forget that he was not a first-round pick and had to earn his spot. I give the guy a lot of credit. What he has is a lot of natural ability.

So, he will be in the HOF as soon as possible.

Other people have not been so lucky.

Can you name the only player to have quarterbacked his team to two SB's and is still NOT in the HOF?

I'll bet you can't.

Others Undrafted

Bill Bates went undrafted in 1983 because the scouts who saw him at the Combine said he was "too slow". He got a chance to try out for the Cowboys anyway. Anyone who has never seen Bates play… well, let's just say you ain't seen nuthin'!

The first game I saw him in, he ran down the field to cover the opening kickoff and hit the returner just a moment after the ball and they all flew ten yards from the point of impact.

This guy played every play like it was the only one that mattered. Many times he knocked himself and the other player unconscious.

He was an immense pleasure to watch and he played all fifteen years of his career with Dallas. After that he went to coaching, including a stretch at Nease High School in Florida when their QB took them to a State Championship. Their QB? Tim Tebow. Yes, the original Tebower learned under one of the best.

Another player who did not impress at the Combine was Everson Walls. The scouts said he was "too slow" – do you notice a disturbing trend here?

He was a fantastic cornerback and led the league in interceptions three years in a row. It has been replicated recently by Ed Reed but no one else was as good as Everson was.

In 1990-91, he went to the Giants and got a Super Bowl ring. And in 1992 he played with Cleveland to finish off his career.

These fellows again proved the metrics being used is wrong.

No Draft? – No Problemo

Among the other undrafted players is Tony Romo. Yes, Dallas' leader came into the league on his own, like so many other great ones.

As you can see, the winners of the Super Bowl are almost evenly split between those guys chosen on the first round and those guys chosen somewhat later, if chosen at all. Steve Young was taken in the supplemental draft and Kurt Warner – who carried two different teams to the Super Bowl – was undrafted.

Adding in all the QBs who have made it to the big game, they are fairly evenly split. There are fifty first rounders who made it to the Super Bowl and fifty from later draft rounds or undrafted who have made it there as well.

Being metrically superior does not ensure making it to the Big One.

There have been only three QBs to take two different teams to the Super Bowl. Craig Morton (1st round draftee) took Dallas there in the 1970 season and then Denver seven years later but lost on both trips.

Kurt Warner (undrafted) took the St. Louis Rams in 1999 and 2000, winning once. Then in 2008 he took the Arizona Cardinals to their first Super Bowl, losing that attempt.

Peyton Manning (another 1st round QB) was the first one to take two teams to the Super Bowl and win with both. He took the Colts there in 2006 and 2009 – winning the first outing – and then the Denver Broncos in 2013 and 2015. The last trip was his second win, making him the first QB to take the Lombardi trophy for two different teams.

Quarterback	Draft Yr	Round Taken	SB's won
Kurt Warner	1994	undrafted	1
Steve Young	1984Sup	1	1
Bart Starr	1956	17	2
Roger Staubach	1964	10	2
Johnny Unitas	1955	9	1
Brad Johnson	1992	9	1
Tom Brady	2000	6	4
Mark Rypien	1986	6	1
Joe Thiesmann	1971	4	1
Joe Montana	1979	3	4
Jeff Hostetler	1984	3	1
Russell Wilson	2012	3	1
Ken Stabler	1968	2	1
Brett Favre	1991	2	1
Drew Brees	2001	2	1
Terry Bradshaw	1970	1	4
Troy Aikman	1989	1	3
Bob Griese	1967	1	2
Jim Plunkett	1971	1	2
John Elway	1983	1	2
Peyton Manning	1998	1	2
Joe Namath	1965	1	1
Len Dawson	1957	1	1
Jim McMahon	1982	1	1
Phil Simms	1979	1	1
Doug Williams	1978	1	1
Trent Dilfer	1994	1	1
Ben Roethlisberger	2004	1	1
Eli Manning	2004	1	1
Ben Roethlisberger	2004	1	1
Aaron Rodgers	2005	1	1
Eli Manning	2004	1	1
Joe Flacco	2008	1	1

Since 1955, there have been a whopping 902 QBs drafted into the NFL, 128 of them being taken in the first round. Of those 128 so chosen, only 7 have made it to the Hall of Fame and three of those seven were all in the first round in 1983: John Elway, Jim Kelly, and Dan Marino.

1983 seems to have been a rather illustrious year but most other years do not have such storybook endings.

Nine undrafted QBs made it to the Pro Bowl in their career but only one has been inducted into the Hall of Fame: Kurt Warner.

You will no doubt have noticed that the draft rounds in some years exceed the seven rounds we usually have at the present. Before 1960 there were 30 rounds and in that year it was reduced to 20. In 1967, it was reduced again to 17 rounds.

In 1977 in was reduced to twelve and in 1994 was finally reduced to the seven rounds we are familiar with.

Perhaps they were merely attempting to increase their odds at not getting any draft busts?

Lessons Learned?

I seriously doubt my observations are going to change the way the scouts and coaches work. Each of them have their "bible", their set of metrics that seem to be chapter and verse in their dogma of what makes a player successful.

That the number of draft busts mounts every year – faster than the number of raging success stories – seems meaningless to these people. The agents for the players love to tout the metrics, the scouts and coaches live by the metrics, and the fans love to argue everything about the numbers.

Numbers are easy.

Numbers are concise.

Wins, losses, yards gained, number of completions, numbers of interceptions… Now they even have the QB rating for every quarterback in every game – even broken down by quarters to feed out hunger for such things.

Numbers rule.

The indefinable qualities that truly define leadership and champions will forever take a back seat because there's no way to base an argument on that stuff.

And who wants the water cooler chats to get all touchy-feely, huh?

PART SIX
A HISTORY OF MISERY

I was not around at the time of the sport's creation although my grandchildren seem to think otherwise.

Football has been around since the nineteenth century and was originally a sport between various institutes of higher learning. Although, as time progressed, the collegial sport and "higher learning" seem to have gone separate directions. I won't bore anyone here with the complete history of the game as there are many competent volumes already out there on the subject. Even a few, I have been told, that were not subsidized by the NFL.

The first American football game was played on November 6, 1869 between Rutgers and Princeton. The game was played between two teams of 25 players each, used a round ball, and resembled a combination of rugby and soccer in its rules; the ball could not be picked up or carried, but it could be kicked or batted with the feet, hands, head or sides, with the ultimate goal of advancing it into the opponent's goal.

Rutgers won the game 6-4. Their dominance did not last too long.

Collegiate play continued for several years in which matches were played using the rules of the host school. Representatives of Yale, Columbia, Princeton and Rutgers met on October 19, 1873 to create a standard set of rules for all schools to adhere to. Teams were set at 20 players each, and fields of 400 by 250 feet were specified. Harvard abstained from the conference, as they favored a rugby-style game that allowed running with the ball.

An 1875 Harvard-Yale game played under rugby-style rules was observed by two impressed Princeton athletes. These players introduced the sport to Princeton, a feat the Professional Football Researchers Association compared to "selling refrigerators to Eskimos." Princeton, Harvard, Yale and Columbia then agreed to intercollegiate play using a form of rugby union rules with a modified scoring system. These schools formed the Intercollegiate Football Association, although Yale did not officially join until

1879. Yale player Walter Camp, now regarded as the "Father of American Football," secured rule changes in 1880 that reduced the size of each team from 15 to 11 players and instituted the snap to replace the chaotic and inconsistent scrum.

It should also be noted that Walter Camp was a member of Skull and Bones. Can anyone detect a sinister conspiracy involving football?

Pre-Snyder Redskins

The Redskins story began in the city of Boston in 1932. They eventually moved from the New England town as a sort of a foreshadowing of the greatness to visit them in the form of Tom Brady's team, formerly known as the Patriots.

After changing their name from the "Boston Braves" to the "Washington Redskins", they quite naturally looked for another place to play… preferably some place called "Washington" so their new name would be meaningful. The place they found was the nation's capital and so the name change stuck. Perhaps if they had left it as it was, there would be less controversy surrounding the team today. Still, it would have been odd for the team in Washington, D.C., – or rather Ashburn, VA, or Landover, MD – to be called the Boston Braves.

Preston Marshall, owner of the team, was not concerned with the name or any derogatory connotations. He was a racist. He refused to add black players to his pure white team.

It took a Presidential order from John Kennedy to integrate the Redskins.

Enter Technology

When I first started watching football, there was no such thing as "instant replay". Yes, believe it or not.

And, no, there were no dinosaurs running around the field either.

There were, however, goalposts in the endzone interfering with the runners and pass receivers. There were quite a few games where players got injured colliding with the damned things but year after year they remained.

That is, until someone developed posts strong enough to stand beyond the end zone but lean into it so the goal posts were in the same place for field goals.

That was not the only technology that impacted the game.

There was also this invention called video-tape.

The networks could show a play – in slow motion even – just after it had happened. It took several years before the League decided to incorporate these instant replays into their officiating toolchest.

I don't know if it was the players association or the league offices or even the officiating personnel who objected the most. Whoever it was, they were dragged into the late twentieth century to the blessed relief of all the fans who had gotten tired of all the bad calls by officials by their refusal to utilize technology.

The NFL, technophobes no more.

Watching the Games

The NFL was shown during the season. After that, we were pretty much in the wilderness until the next season.

Then came ESPN and they would re-broadcast games at times, usually only as a lead in to the upcoming season but it was better than nothing.

Then came the NFL channel. Finally, we could feed our addiction to all things football 24/7 anytime we felt the need for a pigskin fix.

And now, with streaming games on the internet, we no longer have to watch only the games that their program directors decide are the ones to see. We can watch any game… well, as long as it happened after 2009.

I keep hounding them to include earlier games – their film department has games all the way back to the 1920's, maybe not complete of course, but… – yet my needs seem to be far down on their list of "To Do's".

Guess I'm not that big a fan in their eyes.

PART SEVEN
NO DODGING THIS DRAFT

In times of dire need, a draft is instituted to call up young men to the service of their country. Some decide to avoid service and simply dodge the draft. But that's politics and unimportant to this volume.

The football draft, on the other hand, is where the college players push and shove to get in line for a chance to play. And there are far more people wanting to be drafted than is allowed by the league. For that reason, they also have a supplemental draft.

In ancient times, each team would have to send scouts into the collegiate system to seek out these soon-to-be-greats and let their team know who was best suited to fit their needs. With more teams came more scouts, all tripping over themselves and making a mess for the colleges.

Then came The Combine. This was a nifty little invention that put most the scouts out of business, or at least put them all in the same spot tripping over each other and not clogging up the college campuses. Rather than have several scouts attempting to evaluate different players on paper and their own subjective interpretations, they now bring all the players to one location. Now through a particular set of metrics, it requires only a single scout for each team to evaluate different players on paper and their own subjective interpretations.

Progress is, oh, so sweet, no?

The Draft Bust

One thing most teams, players, scouts, and coaches avoid like the plague is the "Draft Bust", the player that looked so good on paper and on display at the Combine but turns out to be a train wreck when he gets to the team facility.

Let's face it, not all players have what it takes to be a professional football player.

And it may not be just a personality clash, or hidden drug-related problems, anger issues, violence issues, alien-abduction issues, spousal issues, extravagant lifestyles, boisterous natures, and the like, it could also be the unluckiness of being injury prone.

Some players have seen the glitzy lifestyles of the marquee names in the league and want that for themselves. When the big payday arrives they are far more ready to get on with living large than with working 24/7 to stay fit and hone their game. Fortunately, the vast majority of rookies have a better head on their shoulders.

I mentioned the young man chosen in the NBA draft several years ago who didn't do much of anything after signing.

Not all draft busts are of that caliber. Many really want to do good and make a long and glorious career but cannot make the transition to the professional game. And do not be fooled, college football is nothing like the NFL. Practically every player I have talked to on the subject says the greatest difference is *speed*. Things in the NFL happen a lot faster during a play than they did in college.

Many players – even some very good players – cannot make that adjustment.

The second-most thing I have heard mentioned is the variables. Every position has built-in modes of operation but they are trained that in situation "A" you do this and in situation "B" you do this. And each variation has sub-variations, called "reads", that make the whole thing a lot more complex.

It is a heck of a lot to remember. Many of them probably wish they were back in the sandlot where the huddle was all about where to go to catch the ball. Nothing fancy, just go out and wait for the ball.

It seems a shame that the Combine does not test for their abilities in this area a little more as it seems to be the make/break plateau of professionalism in the sport.

Undrafted

There are some players who – for some reason or another – do not get drafted. Some just shrug their shoulders and get on with life while some keep pursuing the dream.

In recent years, we are seeing more and more of these players entering the league and doing a fine job regardless of what any former scouts might have thought. I suppose it is drive that keeps them going or perhaps that mental acuity to play the game at that level (that "it" factor that the Combine does not seem to address).

I have mentioned a few before like Bill Bates, Kurt Warner, and Tony Romo. Another pretty good player was Wes Welker. He played with several different teams but made the biggest splash with New England. When they cut him in favor of Julian Edelman (recently drafted) Wes went to Denver and helped Peyton get to the Super Bowl. He was a pretty good player even if "too small" by all the scouts' estimates.

Another thing about it happening more than it used to, the draft used to be much larger… 30 rounds. Today it is seven!

That's quite a reduction and all those hopefuls out of college have to find another way to break into the league. Most, I guess, hang up their cleats and move onto their second career choice.

One accountant I worked with several years ago, went to the Redskins camp every year to try out as a walk-on. One year he was lucky enough to make it to their practice squad for a while but every year, he still tries out.

It is a hard dream to give up.

Diamonds in the Rough

There are quite a few players taken in the first round of the draft that disappear all too quickly. Some, like Peyton and his brother Eli, are quite capable of sustaining a high level of production over many years.

Every now and then we see a remarkable thing: someone drafted in the later rounds of the draft, unheralded, not the usual household-name college quarterback, steps up and wows the crowd.

Sometimes it is the size of the college they attended and sometimes it is simply because they did not seek out the spotlight as so many have. They take their time, quietly learning what they need to for the team and when the time is ready... BAM!

Neither Joe Montana nor Tom Brady was taken in the first (or second) round of the draft. All but one team seemed to have them completely off the radar but many would later wish they had been more prescient. Both of them have done remarkably well in their careers.

Many teams' fans had wished their team had been smart enough/quick enough, whatever, to get such a good player but no one has found the perfect formula yet. No one has yet determined those one or two factors that are really important.

Yes, *That* Subject Again

Regardless your personal feelings about Tim Tebow and the baggage he carts around, no one can deny that he is a catalyst for a team. For all the problems he had with mechanics and his poor passer-rating, the fellow won games. And I have always thought it is more about winning games that looking good while doing so.

Many analysts tell us that he looks poor in practice. If we were interested only in having the man practice from now until doomsday, I think that would be a big deal. But he is supposed to *play* the game not merely practice.

I have seen many, many players look really good in practice but cannot seem to pull it off during a game. That's what the Combine does, looks for people with good mechanics, nice footwork, and so forth. Apparently, most early scouts of Brady said he ran like a duck and gave him bad marks for it. He doesn't run much... he doesn't have to. What were those guys thinking?

In public education, we often hear about the kids that are really smart, read a lot, write well, and can answer any question during classroom discussion, but they have trouble when taking tests.

That's the same problem I see in the Tebow situation: it is not about the ability of the test-taker but the usefulness of the test.

Sure, Tebow's playoff win against Pittsburgh was a short-lived run, but far better players and teams have gone down in Foxborough.

It doesn't mean Tebow or the team was bad. Heck, they had just defeated the Pittsburgh Steelers, a much higher seed in the AFC. Give the man a little credit, please.

Matches Made in Heaven

Dan Marino was drafted by the Miami Dolphins and stayed there throughout his career. He took the team to the Super Bowl in his second season there but lost. He never made it back to the big game even though he had some great years statistically.

Terry Bradshaw was drafted by the Pittsburgh Steelers and he remained there for the duration of his career. He was able to get to the big game four times and won every time.

Tom Brady has only been on the Patriots. I cannot imagine he would ever go somewhere else any more than I can conceive of the team wanting to get rid of him until he retires.

Most players today, it seems, move around the league from one team to another and it is harder to identify a team by one player, be it the QB or another position.

Players I admired on one team I followed, moved elsewhere. Some I tried to follow – Patrick Ramsey, Eddie Royal, Tim Tebow, RG3, Joe Montana, Wes Welker, Brett Favre, and a host of others.

It was not easy in previous years but with the online NFL capability of watching any game I want, it is a lot easier to follow these guys week-to-week.

Matches Made Elsewhere

John Elway was taken in the first round by the Baltimore Colts. He really did not want to be on the East Coast. After some tense moments, he was traded to Denver where he had a remarkable career.

Atlanta drafted Brett Favre but the coach was not pleased. Jerry Glanville did not like the young man and thought he was a terrible choice. After seeing him on the field a couple of times – shades of Montana, Brady, and others – he felt confirmed in his estimation of the fellow and traded him to Green Bay. Good thing for Green Bay, huh?

San Diego drafted Eli Manning as the #1 draft choice in 2004 but Eli balked. He had mentioned earlier that he would refuse to go to San Diego and he stuck by that statement. Eventually, San Diego was able to switch drafted players with the New York Giants. Eli went to New York while Philip Rivers was the young man who went west. It seems to have worked out for both of them and I think San Diego has stopped booing Eli whenever he comes to play (but I might be wrong).

Eli really did not want to be in the same conference as his brother, Peyton. When Peyton was cut loose by Indianapolis a few years back, he refused out of hand all offers from teams in the NFC. The Redskins made on offer – I'm sure Snyder was salivating like crazy – but playing for Washington would pit brother against brother twice a year and that was something the Manning boys would like to avoid. Peyton remained in the AFC leaving Eli as the lone Manning for the NFC.

Why players hold out against some teams are not always as obvious as the few listed and why some coaches have it out for some players seems even more mysterious. When Tebow was bought up by the Jets organization, the coach could barely hide his dislike for the player and refused to put him in even while the team's season went down in flames.

Some of the people involved in this "team sport" do not seem to have a team mentality. They treat it more like…

Well, like a business.

PART EIGHT
PRIMA DONNAS

There are a lot of fans who dote on the quarterbacks. These guys are the high profile positions as team leaders. They usually get more press, more glory, more attention than the other players.

And, so it would seem, a lot of them act like they are something special.

Most long-time Cowboy fans know about Clint Longley. He was the backup to Roger Staubach for a time. In one particular Thanksgiving Day game, with the 'Boys faltering and Staubach knocked out of the game, in waltzed Longley to lead the team to a very impressive victory.

Supposedly, he and Roger got along quite nicely. The next year, however, tensions seemed to get a little raw. Various versions of the events have come out over the years – Staubach called Clint out for verbally abusing another team member, or Clint was uptight because new recruit Danny White was edging him out of the backup spot, or some more personal reasons – something led Clint to walk up behind Roger in the locker room and punch him in the side of the face without warning.

He was, of course, immediately released by the team.

Roger Staubach has always seemed a fairly square guy but there were some of those present at that incident who seemed to think Roger somehow got what he deserved. I don't know and perhaps we will never know what really happened but… Come on, who deserves a sucker punch like that, huh?

I lived in Hollywood for several years and learned that to make it in that industry you have to be a heavy-handed self-promoter. If your ego is not at least the size of, say, Cleveland, you'll never make it in the industry.

Perhaps it is no different in football as well.

I remember hearing Vince Young say, after his first season, that he was thinking of retiring because the game was not what he had expected. And this past off-season, Robert Griffin III made a similar comment about the game. Of course, most people focused on the part where he supposedly claimed he was the best quarterback in the league (it was taken out of context, of course) but I was struck by what he said earlier in the statement that the game was not what he had thought. It was run far more like a business and had its share of machinations, manipulations, politicking and backstabbing.

Yes, this profession can eat you alive if you're not watching out. Non-self-promoters beware!

Not the Only Prima Donna

Another position that seems to garner a lot of the spotlight is the Head Coach. I've seen so many different sorts come and go from that position over the years as well.

One of my early favorites was John Madden when he led the heyday of the Raiders. He was always so animated, waving his arms around and practically frothing from the mouth. Yes, he was excitable.

Bum Phillips (father of coach Wade Phillips) always wore his ten-gallon cowboy hat to every game, except those inside a domed venue. He always said his Mother taught him proper manners: never wear a hat indoors.

A very different sort of hat was wielded by Tom Landry the first and ever coach (so it seemed) of the Cowboys. And he very rarely showed any emotion whatsoever. He scored and he was blank. They blew it and he was again blank. Once in a Super Bowl, an interception by his QB actually drew a wince from him. But that was about it. He was very detached from the game it seemed.

And then there's Rex Ryan. His tenure with the Jets included some of the most interesting press conferences I've ever seen. It seemed that was the only thing interesting during his tenure there. We were always assured a good chuckle.

Except during the period when Tebow was with the team. Again, it was obvious the coach was trying to "prove he was right" by sabotaging the entire team – and the fans – all just to insure the object of his ire never got a shot to show what he could do.

When Tebow tried out for the Eagles, the stands were packed with Tebow fans. I always wonder if Chip Kelly might have been maintained there if he had utilized the fellow.

Another colorful coach well known for his rants during postgame press sessions was Jim Mora, Peyton Manning's first NFL coach. Who could possibly forget his marvelous "Playoffs?!" rant. If you've never seen it (or heard it) check it out on YouTube. I've seen several versions there, shortened ones as well as the complete rant.

My favorite coach from all my years of watching football has to be Bill Belichick. This guy is creative, insightful, and a veritable genius. Yes, he sometimes pushes the envelope a little too far, too hard, but he's always staying innovative.

Good Leadership Skills

Some of the QBs are seemingly less self-centered than others.

In far too many games I saw Dan Marino throw an errant pass and he got mad at the receiver. Sure, there are probably times the receiver and QB are not on the same page – or the same play – but I cannot believe Dan was 100% blameless on every occasion even though that's the way he acted.

I like to see the QB groan after a bad play and tap his own chest as if to say, "Sorry. That goof was on me." The better players do this. They may not all be the better QBs but they are definitely the better players.

Troy Aikman was generally soft spoken. A lot of people think he was one of the greatest QBs of all time. I believe even Troy knows it was not his skills that won all those games, or three Super Bowls. I think a number of other QBs would have done that good given what he had to work with.

What am I talking about?

I remember one season where Troy was out on injury for four games… the Cowboys won every game with the backup. Later, Michael Irvin was out for three weeks. They won every game.

Toward the end of the season, Emmitt Smith was out on injury for three games. The Cowboys lost all three games.

That should show you who the most valuable player was.

Something similar happened in New England.
Brady was out for an entire season due to a back injury.
Without him, the team still made the playoffs. They are much better with him, I believe, but without Coach Belichick the Patriots would probably tank.
Bill is the vital cog in the Patriots organization.

Going All Hollywood

Aside from the Coach and QB, there are often other prima donnas in the game. These characters get the extra attention because of their off field antics and their sometimes very vocal opinions of other teams and other players.
Terrell Owens was a marvelous example of this and, unfortunately, his mouth is probably what ended his career.
Richard Sherman is another who likes to drop sound bites to the press. He and Revis are probably the most well-known currently.
That these mouths are sometimes shut down by losing a game does not seem to hamper their continuance of the yak. Some people just don't know when to keep quiet. (Hmm, sounds a bit like me, I think…)
The better, more professional players, let their actions on the field do their speaking for them. They came to play football, not hog any spotlight.
And then there's Chad Ochocinco…
'Nuff said.

When Is It About the Game?

The chest-pounding of players and coaches as well as the dismissive comments made about the opposition in the lead-up to a game is fairly universal and I am pretty sure it went on during medieval jousting contests and may even have been a common feature when our ancestors competed with those in a neighboring cave.

When the caterwauling does not focus on individuals or personalities, it can be very healthy. Like RG3 said in an interview, he has to think that he's the best in the game or he could not go out on the field and attempt to BE that guy.

A lot of people took the quote all wrong and thought the guy was saying he was saying he was better than anyone, even Brady and Peyton. If a QB took the field against Brady and thought "I can never beat this guy!" then he has already lost the game.

Confidence is healthy.

Confidence is a game changer.

Keeping a mindset focused on the positives of your ability and your preparation – especially when shared among all the members of the team – is a key factor in becoming a winning team.

I'm sure you've noticed players on the sideline who look demoralized and defeated by the middle of the third quarter; to them, the game is already lost and they can hardly wait to simply get out of the stadium.

Confidence is a benefit, trash talking not so much, especially when the trash talking focused on individuals and personalities rather than on team – and this is, after all, a team sport. No one person can win the game just as no one person can lose it.

Not singling out individuals is what keeps the attitude healthy.

It is a team sport, not just about the loud mouth on the sideline.

Really Bad Coaching

I mentioned that I admired Belichick and his attempts to stretch the limits at times. Some of his actions may have been ill-advised but none of them holds a candle to what one coach did.

No, not the guy who would stand on the sideline and trip opposing players running past – though that sort of behavior should get you banned from life from the NFL – there was another coach whose behavior was so despicable… that he's still working in the NFL.

Yeah, deflating footballs will draw the unending ire of the football gods but setting up a hit squad to intentionally maim or otherwise do intentional damage on other players seems to be the thing of a minor hand-slap.

Yes, in a professional league that gives tremendous amount of lip-service to player safety, the mastermind of mayhem still has a job.

Gregg Williams was a much-touted defensive coach when he came to Washington. Soon, I noticed that our defensive leader, LaVar Arrington wasn't playing as much as he once did.

Apparently, he could not master the "defensive scheme" Williams had brought to Washington. Yes, Williams could not find a way to utilize the best defensive player we had, so he simply benched the fellow.

I will be bringing up this subject again as it relates to my earlier complaints of the metrics coaches and scouts use. This sort of crap really should stop… but it won't simply because we have so few Belichicks and so damned many bean counters thinking all parts of the universe can be reduced to a spreadsheet.

Anyway, a year after Williams left Washington he went to work in New Orleans and that's where the word came out about his "bounty system". Yes, bonuses galore if you could take an opponent out of the game and bigger bonuses if you could take them out for the season.

I suppose he thought it was nothing more than offering an incentive program for his squad to "play better"… although "play dirtier" might be a better label. Apparently, there was not enough evidence of his doing similar actions during his time in Washington but here near the beltway, we have heard stories.

So Kyle Shanahan and Gregg Williams are still coaching.

Is it any wonder I can only scratch my head at times?

PART NINE
COACH 'EM UP

I'm sure everyone is familiar with the play diagrams used in football. You can see them in movies, commercials and occasionally in photos about the football facilities.

The first time I saw one like this I thought, those guys on the right side turn and run along the line to the left side?? How exactly does this work? Won't they run into all sorts of people?
　　Well, I watched the offensive line on quite a few plays and got to see this thing work out in real time. They don't always block straight to the front!! What an amazing discovery. It was like poetry in motion.
　　Of course, sometimes, the defensive linemen can sometimes disrupt this sort of thing but that's another story.

A Novel Notion, Perhaps...

One idea I toyed with several years ago was a way to reduce the paperwork. Yes, my own paperwork reduction act [patent pending].

Some of these teams have playbooks that are simply massive.

You know, the eighty-five different formations the offensive squad can take to run a play. And each of those formations have a wide variety of plays that can be run from that particular set.

The wild variations have come about to psyche out the defense. The defense now has to watch all your game film so they will know which formation leads to which plays. And they have to be ready for detecting which alignment your team takes and what sending various players in motion could mean.

It's all very technical – I am sure – and has to be constantly adapting, changing, morphing, because defenses DO learn what you're doing.

And so often we see the confusion of the team running the play. The QB has to stop what he is doing to reposition one of the players who had remembered the play wrong or gotten mixed up with where they were supposed to be. Many times, timeouts have to be wasted because not everyone is on the right page.

So, my thought was, why not completely psyche the defense out by taking the very same alignment on *every single play*? First down, third down, doesn't matter. Line up in the same formation every single time and their viewing of all the game films from here to Timbuktu won't matter. They will not be able to read what offensive plays you might run from that formation because you run every stinking play from the same formation.

But, like I said, the patent on this idea is still pending, so keep it under your hat.

Curse You, Chip Kelly!!

Well, it was bound to happen, you know. Someone leaked my idea and Chip Kelly seems to have adapted it for his own use.

Yeah, I know he uses more than the single formation but his playbook has the fewest number of offensive alignments of any team in the NFL.

Since he runs such a fast-paced offense, it was probably a good idea to keep at least some portion of the game simpler rather than more complex.

We'll have to wait and see if the fellow "pulls the trigger" and reduces the number of formations even further... like down to a single one.

If that happens, I might have to start my own investigation... find out who leaked the idea to Coach Kelly. (It couldn't be he read this book, could it? Nah!)

I wonder if Roger would loan me the investigators he used on Deflategate? Yeah, those guys could find... well, surely they might be able to find something even if it is not even tangentially connected to what they were tasked to find.

Omaha

The use of the word "Omaha" has been noted by many and the explanations of same have been given by countless talking heads, including Peyton himself.

He told us that it usually means a change in the play although at other times it doesn't. If it was a running play, it would change to a pass but if it had been a passing play it was changed to a run... most of the time, anyway. Seems like a real clear and straightforward explanation to me, at least as long as you recall that Peyton was a master of tongue-in-cheek.

Its use certainly kept people guessing throughout the Sheriff's career and I would imagine he liked to throw it in on occasion just to really confuse the defense.

I have watched plenty of his games over the years and I still cannot see anything consistent in the usage. But then I might be looking for the wrong things.

We may never know, beyond its primary position in Nebraska, just what the word actually meant.

To anyone.

Trick Plays

Like most other fans, I love to see trick plays being used. Fake punts, fake field goals, and the like but they have not been used very much in the professional sport. Why? Probably because they so often fail.

When they work, the coach looks like a genius.

When they fail, the coach looks like a fool.

And no coach really wants that so much, except if you are intentionally looking for laughs like Rex Ryan is famous for.

The one trick play that seems to still find a widespread use is the "wild cat" where the QB lines up somewhere other than where he should be and the ball is put in play in another's hands, usually a running back who simply takes off running.

In essence, this is the same sort of thing Tebow did a lot as QB. He just as often became a running back when he got the ball. RG3 used to do this a lot as well.

I have often wondered – returning to my concept at the start of this chapter about a standardized offense formation – if the team had two players like Tebow and RG3 and started them both in the pistol formation (side by side behind center) how much would it mess with the heads of the defense.

Either person could either pass or run with the ball or even lateral it to the other guy to run or pass the ball.

It would certainly be a bit confusing to defenses especially if every play started out exactly the same.

But, like *that's* ever going to happen in the NFL, huh?

Chatting 'Em Up

One of my favorite coach interviews after a game was Jim Mora's famous "playoffs?!!" segment. One of the most depressing was watching Cam Newton after his Super Bowl loss in SB50. It was as if someone had sucked all the life right out of the fellow. I'm sure the team's PR people had coached him in how to act the gracious loser in front of the cameras but anyone could see his heart really wasn't in it. Some people said he was a sore loser... all I saw was a young man who really thought he was going to hoist the Lombardy until reality smacked him upside the head.

He was being a little too human for some people. Yes, he took it personal rather than treating it like a business. You could almost hurt with the guy.

Most of the time, however, the players respond very predictably to the routine reporter questions. Watching these things I find counterproductive. I've seen so many over the years that I can give their responses before they do. Losing teams always say they simply "got outplayed", that the other team was "better-prepared", and they saw a lot of "room for improvement" on their own "preparation and skills".

I miss Jim Mora.

Chatting 'Em Up

At the end of last season, we get a story about an old Patriot problem being far, far worse than the NFL let on. Probably not in the way you would expect, however.

Frank Schwab claimed that Goodell had gone easy on the Pats for Spygate and hid how bad it really was and that's why he threw the book at them for deflategate.

The Patriots responded to the ESPN story. Here's the team's statement, via CSNNE:

"The New England Patriots have never filmed or recorded another team's practice or walk through. The first time we ever heard of such an accusation came in 2008, the day before Super Bowl XLII, when the Boston Herald reported an allegation from a disgruntled former employee. That report created a media firestorm that extended globally and was discussed incessantly for months. It took four months before that newspaper retracted its story and offered the team a front and back page apology for the damage done. Clearly, the damage has been irreparable. As recently as last month, *over seven years after the retraction and apology was issued*, ESPN issued the following apology to the Patriots for continuing to perpetuate the myth: 'On two occasions in recent weeks, SportsCenter incorrectly cited a 2002 report regarding the New England Patriots and Super Bowl XXXVI. That story was found to be false, and should not have been part of our reporting. We apologize to the Patriots organization.'

"This type of reporting over the past seven years has led to additional unfounded, unwarranted and, quite frankly, unbelievable allegations by former players, coaches and executives. None of which have ever been substantiated, but many of which continue to be propagated. The New England Patriots are led by an owner whose well-documented efforts on league-wide initiatives – from TV contracts to preventing a work stoppage – have earned him the reputation as one of the best in the NFL. For the past 16 years, the Patriots have been led by one of the league's all-time greatest coaches and one of its all-time greatest quarterbacks. It is disappointing that some choose to believe in myths, conjecture and rumors rather than giving credit for the team's successes to Coach Belichick, his staff and the players for their hard work, attention to detail, methodical weekly preparation, diligence and overall performance."

Okay, Brady/Belichick-haters, the ball's in your court.

PART TEN
SCHEMERS AND DREAMERS

I have a very low opinion of those who value systems and schemes over people. Leadership is not getting people to do what you want but getting people to buy into your vision and do *their damnedest* to get it done.

It's easy to say that everyone wants to win – who in a competitive business does not want that? – but where's the humanity?

Everson Walls was cut by Jimmy Johnson, the Dallas coach, for visiting with the opposing team players after the game.

Another coach, defensive "guru"/"felon" Greg Williams, benched a player for helping an opposing player off the ground after a play. This, of course, fits in with Williams' bounty-mindedness. Why the league allowed him to continue coaching astonished me. Does Goodell think that only players can give the league a bad name? Coaches who seem to have lost all contact with reality can do that as well.

Williams was with us in Washington for a time and shows the type of insanity I'm talking about: schemes and systems.

Here's how this came about.

When you have a lackluster or sub-par group of people, the way to improve their output is to put in place a system that requires little or no thought or input from the people. The phrase *deus ex machina* comes to mind.

And there's nothing wrong with this. Many of the players in the NFL are functional – surely better than most college players on the average – but not all of them are *great*.

These people can use a system to best advantage. I'm not saying these people are stupid – they are far from it – but they do not have that spark of ingenuity that lifts some of their number to greatness. There were cornerbacks in the league that were much faster than

Everson Walls, could leap higher than Everson, but obviously did not *want it as much as* Everson.

That's the part that cannot be schemed or systematized: the gift of originality. Trying to force someone of that caliber into a square hole is not only poor judgement, it shows a complete inability to understand coaching.

Greg Williams came to Washington with this great "system" of his and he encountered a brilliant player already here: Lavar Arrington. This young man had already broken records with his intuitive understanding of the game and his marvelous physical gifts.

Greg Williams insisted the system was more important and would not bend any of his scheme to include Arrington. Eventually the coach got rid of his little troublemaker and forced the scheme on the team.

Later he took his marvelous system to New Orleans, and we all know what happened there.

Lessons unlearned, many coaches still prefer schemes over people.

Anyone who has spent time at the crap table in Vegas knows that you keep placing bets on the line, hoping someone comes along with a hot hand and can start rolling a string of numbers. You don't simply place a bet or two and – when nothing wins – walk away from the table. You wait for a roller to get hot.

You do not tell the hot-hand to step away from the table so everyone can keep losing money. The hot hand is what you are praying for.

The same should be true for football. There are plenty of very good football players out there and so very few of the exceptional quality.

To take exceptional quality players – whether they are QBs like RG3 or Tebow or defensive players like LaVar Arrington – and tell them to adjust to fit in the system. I don't care how "great" your system is but if it does not *account for genius* then all you are ever going to get is a mediocre team.

I cannot stress this enough…

And nobody ever seems to listen enough.

Oh well.

Real World, not Fantasy Football

It's all about the X's and O's they say. All about the game plan.

Those people who have at least the slightest grounding in living on this planet know that "game plans" rarely turn out as envisioned. Corporations check the trends and set up their projections for the future of their business, the market, the changing consumer base and so forth.

Then some knucklehead comes up with a completely off-the-wall idea/concept/product and all the days and weeks spent on that marvelous "game plan" go right out the window.

Behemoths and other dinosaurs spend far too much time and money on planning a continuance of mediocrity and how to achieve a degree of dominance over it. And it would all work out just splendidly if everyone would just stay within the structure as planned.

Many times we have seen athletes that excelled in the college arena but cannot make the transition to the professional grade. Some can make the shift but others are found sadly lacking. The first thing most of the rookies have mentioned is the speed of the game. Professional football moves a lot faster than the college version. Sort of like the difference between playing "Asteroids" and playing "Halo".

That Special Feeling

Specialization is key to the game. In the sandlot football you played as a kid, the players just "went out" for the ball. "Go long", "cut across", and so forth were about all the planning that was done in the huddle.

In the professional game, each play has very specific moves for every player on the team and – to add a little more complexity to the game – adjustments that will be made on the fly while the play is developing. If the defense does X then adjust by doing Y; if the defense does Y, then adjust by doing Z. And it works really well when all the players on the team can see the defensive adjustments, read them the same way, and use the correct adjustments.

Such stuff takes an awful lot of practice, let me tell you!

One would think that being a guard would be similar to a tackle – both are offensive linemen, right? – and one should be fairly interchangeable. In the professional sport today a right tackle often has trouble changing to left tackle. Wide receivers sometimes cannot transition to the slot position. Specialization is key.

And then there are what I call the hybrids. Natural talents that do not fit into a single place in the scheme of a defense or offense. Trying to get these people to conform to a system is a waste of everyone's time. It's like trying to shave the round sides off a peg and force it into a square hole.

Such natural talents are actually quite rare. It's not like they appear in the draft every year but they are there and – sadly – many of them wash out of the league quite early because too many of the coaches are sold on the idea of schemes over the idea of talent. If the player cannot conform to the scheme, forget them. Trying to design a game plan around a few special players – no matter how talented – seems too much trouble.

Yet, the way things are, most players are talented athletes and can adjust to different schemes, if and where needed. It would seem almost a no-brainer to adjust the scheme to accommodate the truly gifted.

Yeah, I know, I'm whispering in a hurricane.

Keeping in Shape

Playing in a sport at the "professional level" is a lot of hard work.

I've seen the players working out, preparing themselves for a game, and you don't usually seeing any slacking off. The coaches are not there to drive the guys into their workouts, the players already know what is required of them and most of them workout all year round to stay as close to "game shape" as they can.

I played tennis competitively (many, many years ago) and practiced four to five hours a day every day, rain or shine. My brother and I would take a snow shovel to the court and clear it so we could play. We did not have access to an indoor court so we did what we could. We found that playing in adverse conditions sharpened our reflexes even more than playing in perfect conditions.

When my brother was not available, I would practice alone. I avoided hitting the ball against a smooth wall – as I see people doing at many tennis facilities – as the ball comes back where you would expect it to; angular momentum and trigonometric angles being what they are. I would use a brick wall. The ball would often hit the rough brick or the angle between bricks where the mortar was and bounce back in an unexpected direction.

It quickened the reflexes.

But that's enough of that. What I am saying is that professional football players know they have to be in shape to play and they work hard at it. The coach doesn't need to tell them to do so. The coach is there to watch them and point out ways to get better at whichever position it is they are preparing for.

Most of the players I know are not slackers. They are fine-tuned and quite capable.

They don't need a coach to get them there.

They need the coach to take them beyond that point.

Adjustments on the Fly

Generally speaking, the only player a team makes adjustments for is the quarterback. You know, the prima donna of the team. Sometimes, though, the team won't even go that far.

In Denver, 2009, when the starting quarterback went down, John Fox sent in the backup whose style was radically different. Unfortunately for many (and to the eternal disgust of John Elway) this backup was able to win. Coach Fox had to adjust the game-plan to match his new starter but most of the players could easily adjust to the new game plan. In this way they were able to get the team into the playoffs and to beat the top-seeded wildcard team in the first round.

I am certain it was a great relief to Elway that Peyton Manning became available at the end of the season so they could dump Tebow – an unnecessary parting of ways – and a few years later get rid of that offensive Coach Fox for putting Tebow in the game in the first place.

Now at Chicago, I am surprised Fox hasn't called up Tebow to try out. The Bears certainly need something to kick them into gear.

Some Owners Can't Think Their Way Out of a Box Either

Sure, the Redskins fans moan under the cruel fates that have given them an owner as miserable as Dan Snyder, but they are not alone. Jim Irsay, the Colts owner, broke the hearts of his teams fans when he got rid of Peyton. Later, of course, he was suspended for having one too many DUI's.

Other owners try the patience of their fans as well.

Wayne Weaver, first owner of the Jaguars, refused to buckle to outraged fans who wanted to at least give Tebow a shot. He soon sold the team. Shahid Khan purchased the team in January 2012 and he seemed even less interested in Tebow, if such a thing was possible, when he was cut by Denver.

Many owners around the league have been a thorn in the side of the fans.

When Bidwell brought the Cardinals to Phoenix, the games were played at Sun Devil Stadium in Tempe, Arizona, where it was illegal to sell beer. Fans didn't like that. Nor were they fond of the highest priced seats in the league.

That situation changed in a few years. Not because Bidwell lowered his prices but because Dan Snyder came along and raised *his*.

Bidwell also was a bit of a skinflint in other regards as well. When they moved to Arizona, they still had a pretty good team but they rather quickly got rid of the better players – "salary cap problems" they claimed – but the real reason was found out rather quickly.

In Bidwell, Snyder has a kindred spirit, if not a mentor.

It seems a shame there aren't more owners like the Patriots' Mr. Kraft.

Seeing Bigger Pictures

Just this morning, ides of August in 2016, I read a fascinating article by NFL Analyst Bucky Brooks about Elway's Contrarian approach to team building. Apparently, Elway has had a revelation – yes, even while he had Peyton in the driver's seat – that the team was more important than the QB.

Peyton already knew this. A couple of times in his career he has opted for a *cut in pay* to help the team get better staffed. Yes, and Tom Brady has done this as well. Either of those two could have commanded even more money than they got but chose instead to help the team.

What a concept, no?

And Elway seems to have finally figured this out. That is why he let the unproven Osweiler go instead of throwing a ton of cash at him. And Ozzie opener for Houston looked pretty bad – but, hey, it's still pre-season!!

Of course, I still don't think it in any way has softened Elway's take on Tebow.

That would take, of course, a miracle.

PART ELEVEN
THE COMMISH

Since the inception of the league, there have only been nine commissioners – eight if you don't count the one interim guy.

NFL Commissioners
1920-21   Jim Thorpe
1921-39   Joseph Carr
1939-41   Carl Storck
1941-46   Elmer Layden
1946-59   Bert Bell
1959-60   Austin Gunsel [interim]
1960-89   Pete Rozelle
1989-06   Paul Tagliabue
2006-now   Roger Goodell

In years and seasons past, there was little talk about the Commissioner. He kept to himself and kept a fairly low profile. The first NFL Commissioner was Jim Thorpe, an amazing Native American athlete, although he was gone before the introduction of the Redskins team.

Holy Batman, It's the Commish!

In the history of the NFL, there have been some larger than life power brokers but none seem to hold a candle to the current commish, Roger Goodell. Son of a US Senator from New York (the fellow appointed to finish Robert F. Kennedy's term after the latter's assassination – See? Yet another conspiracy connection!! I'll get into this stuff later…). The Senator was not even a gleam in his own father's eye when the NFL was formed.

In recent times, Goodell has come under some harsh scrutiny for the uneven application of fines and discipline he hands down. A lot of fans are just about fed up with the guy.

So, why do the owners keep him?

Because, he has his eyes focused on the bigger picture.

Years ago, I took a course in marketing and public relations and found that *any* news – good, bad, or indifferent – is preferable to no news.

One thing Roger has done is having kept the NFL on everyone's mind. All. Year. Long! Even if all they can talk about is how bad Goodell is, they are talking football 24/7, 365.

The anger and interest brings the clicks to NFL websites, sales of NFL equipment, and so forth. He does Tom Brady a bad turn – as in the recent "deflategate" non-scandal – and suddenly everyone's rushing out in support of Brady, the Patriots, and, as it turns out, the NFL. It's all good.

Before Goodell, football used to be "hot" maybe five months a year. With the amazing marketing strides he has made, we have football news and interest… wait for it. All. Year. Long!

Is this guy good or what?

Keeping the Score Straight

After three weeks of watching a recent NFL season I think this tally is what sent Commissioner Goodell over the edge. The score?

REFS 0   REPLACEMENTS -35

And you're probably wondering how could anyone have a negative score? But if you had watched any of the games, it is easy to see how.

As much as the fans complain at the "bad reffing" in so many of the games, Goodell has shown us the error of our ways… or their ways… or somebody's ways! Never were the fans more relieved to see the guys in the zebra stripes run out onto the field. Gone were the shouts of "kill the refs" and, in many places, the guys were greeted with standing ovations.

So, now we have the real refs back and the games can get back to being a contest between the teams on the field rather than a contest between the prima donna coaches and the men in the zebra shirts that were completely unprepared for the "big leagues".

And no longer will we have to worry about the deep pockets of the owners getting even deeper (which they will) and their carping about how much their profits will be cut into (don't worry, they won't)...

At least until the next time the players, the media, the fans, the refs, or Commissioner Goodell decide to try and flex their muscles.

Maybe all those sorts of nuisances should remove themselves from the league and go join the NBA where that sort of behavior seems to be welcomed.

And the rest of us can get back to the really important things about football...

Like the fantasy players and the bounty set-up by certain defensive coordinators – funny, isn't that sort of thing called "offensive" to most sensibilities? – and whether some real teams (remember those?) will make the playoffs this year?

But, hey, it's only a game, right?

Now Where'd the Replacement Refs Go When We Needed Them?

Later, that same season...

Since the return of the "professional" referees have returned to the NFL games, I have seen some behaviors and calls that seem to show the long shadow of the replacement refs we had to start the season.

The Pittsburgh – New York game yesterday had quite a few "questionable" calls... No, I can't say that. "Questionable" means that given the benefit of the doubt, you could call them right. These calls were just plain wrong. And even with the benefit of going "under the hood" and seeing the play again in slo-mo from multiple angles, they still got it wrong.

It was so bad that many comments on nfl.com implied that it appeared obvious to many that Goodell had "fixed" the game. Well, he did have a meeting earlier in the week with the owners of the Giants... nah!

I don't think it was an attempt to "fix" the game as I am certain the refs could have gotten even worse if they had really been trying to insure a Giants victory.

But even without Goodell's collusion, the game was not called very well.

The game with the Redskins and Carolina did not fare any better, though their officiating crew seem to be cut from the same cloth. It was so bad that on one call, with the Carolina player racing down the sideline, the side judge blew the whistle – apparently thinking the player had stepped out of bounds.

Now, we have been told for years that the whistle ends the play, regardless of what went on before, after, or during. A multitude of officiating sins over the years have been wiped aside because of this all important factor. Here, however, it was the *cause* of the officiating sin.

So, when the whistle blew, most the players stopped the action, except the player running down the sideline. Nobody stopped him – hey, the play was whistled "over", you know? – and he ran for a touchdown. And, yes, it was a touchdown.

When did the magic whistle come to mean so little? (And why haven't I seen the memo?)

The real refs returned after a miserable Monday Night Football game and looked a little rusty the first week out. But rather that getting better, they looked rustier the next week. This weekend, they looked even worse.

I don't think Goodell is using his zombie zebra army to fix any games or to stack the playoff deck, but seems more of the continuing stench from earlier in the season.

Can it be that the replacement refs and these guys are really one any the same? Can it be that the replacement refs never really left us because they are still here in the real zebra outfits?

But that makes even less sense than the game-fixing conspiracy theory and a bit more decidedly south of weird for my taste.

Still, it makes you wonder how badly the replacements could have done in these games. And I cannot believe they could have been any worse than we got.

REFS -22   REPLACEMENTS -35

Replacement Refs Re-Do – update

Greg Rosenthal reporting at nfl.com says "In Sunday's game between the Carolina Panthers and Washington Redskins, the Panthers were incorrectly awarded a touchdown following an inadvertent whistle," an NFL spokeperson said in a statement to CBS Sports.

They say the touchdown should not have counted and the ball should have been placed at the seventeen yard line.

But it does not say if the refs were fined or penalized in any way, like being sent back to replacement ref academy or anything.

And even Mr. Rosenthal reflects on the replacement refs as well: "It is rare to see an entire group of NFL officials melt under pressure like they did in this case. It certainly appeared the officials knew they made a mistake by blowing the whistle, so they tried to correct it, even if that meant going against the rulebook.

"We can only imagine how badly replacement refs would have been crucified had this happened under their watch."

Thanks, NFL, I'm sure that makes the Redskin fans feel a whole lot better about the game, now.

And just how much money are these people making, anyway?

Ah, well, it's a booming business and there's money enough to go around for all of them, I am sure.

It's only a game, right?

Another Season in the Can

Well, it was all over but the Super Bowl and I cannot express how glad I was that lousy season was *over*!

We started out with the lousy reffing of the replacements and finally (!) Roger Goodell pressured them to sign a contract and get the regular refs back on the field. We all heaved a sigh of relief.

Unfortunately, I cannot see that the reffing got any better. All season long, every game I saw, I was wishing the replacement refs were back on the field. Even in the playoffs, it was so miserable that I was praying they would bring them back.

Why?

Simple. With such lousy reffing – and it was as bad as when I played on my junior high team (and that was fifty years ago) – if we only had the replacements still on the field I would *understand* why it was so piss poor.

With the "professional" refs present, you would expect at least a semi-professionally reffed game. But no such luck.

Missed calls, erroneous calls, too damned many ref huddles where they try to figure out what the heck game they are reffing, or what day of the week it is, or what movies are showing on the local theaters, or something!

So, we can now – or at least after just one more game – put this madness behind us and *hope* next season will see the return of the true professional refs.

Maybe it's just that they did not have time at the start of the season to "find their groove". Maybe those first weeks of preseason would have been enough to help these poor guys get into the swing of it.

And, as it turned out, they missed that vital breaking-in period and seemed a little off-kilter, a little out of touch, slightly unbalanced all season long.

I just hope with the off-season that they can regroup and give us a much better season that the one they just finished.

Yeah, I know, you're not supposed to complain about the reffing... if you're an NFL coach, that is, and I am not one of those.

My old high school coach said "the refs can't beat you"... but I don't think he saw anything as lousy as this year's reffing.

Start to finish, it was one for the record books.

And like the fans of all the losing teams say: "Hey, there's always next year."

Even for the refs.

Looking for Scores? Wait for it...

Here it is, Wednesday evening, and I opened up NFL.com to check all the scores from last weeks' games.
From the main page, I clicked the link labeled "SCORES". Should do the trick, right?
Oh, if only it was so easy!!
The page it took me to was one that displayed brightly at the top "WEEK 16".
Only problem, that is the week that is yet to come.
It hasn't happened yet.
It starts tomorrow night with the game with Tennessee at Jacksonville.
But that game *has not happened* yet so naturally there are *NO scores*.
If I had wanted to see a lack of scores I would have clicked that link... well, if there was one. (Note to NFL.com: please add the link to "No Scores" please. Thanks!)
If I had only wanted to know which games were upcoming, I wouldn't even have had to click anything as that data is on a banner across the top of the homepage.
Maybe I'm being a bit too nit-picky here but shouldn't the link for scores actually take you to some scores?

But maybe I'm just a little tired after my long day at work.
And isn't nit-picky what I am all about?
That should not be misconstrued... like Jay Gruden claims his comments about RG3 are. He whined and said his words were being twisted. He really harbors no ill will for the fellow and just wants him to become a better quarterback.
Well, Jay, I don't have to twist your words to know how badly RG3 played in the second half against the Giants after you had your little "pep talk" with him.
Actions speak louder than words, you know.
And you can't complain anybody "twisted" them.

*** UPDATE – the NFL.com people have just released an update to the "No Scores" thing. They are now going to give you the choice to turn off the scores so as to not act as a spoiler.

Although I don't see how that's going to help... If I click on SCORES I think that means that I really want...

Oh, never mind!!

Another PR Fiasco? Au Contraire!

I would be sadly remiss as a football fan if I did not weigh in on "deflategate", as the multi-faceted fiasco is being called.

Brady-haters are cheering the Commish for knocking the fellow down a few pegs even if he did stop short of reversing the Super Bowl win. They think the punishment is a good start for treating Brady.

On the other hand, the Patriot faithful are howling at the grave injustice of it all, especially since the Wells Report contained absolutely no evidence of wrongdoing. They claim Brady is being railroaded.

The majority of the press corps is talking about the adjudication by Goodell is not about the present case but includes all the former shenanigans the Patriots have pulled over the years. In short he is trying to stop the arrogance of the Belichick way of doing things.

Well, at least they are right in one respect, I think. This is all about the past.

No, not the past missteps of the Patriots organization... if I recall correctly, they have been penalized for every one of those things previously. They are being penalized for the missteps of one Roger Goodell, and all the disciplinary missteps he has made over the past season or so.

Goodell claims that the "deflategate" mess, that he claims (without any evidence) was created by the Patriots and as such besmirches the great name of the NFL. They, he crows, have tarnished the legacy... yada yada yada.

Perhaps he is most upset that they have infringed on his territory as "tarnishing the legacy of the NFL" has been mostly in his bailiwick for the past couple of years. And, if I might add, he has done an exemplary job of mucking things up.

So all the Brady-haters can gloat – who cares? the guy will be in the Hall of Fame as soon as he's eligible – and all the Patriotic folks can rail – the penalties will probably be overturned by an impartial panel, just like all the other proclamations on high by the Commish – because it all comes together to serve the major purpose behind what Goodell really does extremely well:

It keeps the NFL in the news, center stage, being talked about. And, all things being equal, that's really what is most important to Goodell, Robert Kraft, Tom Brady, all the other owners and all the other players.

The NFL is front and center in the news, in chats around the water cooler, and on a billion-and-one blogs (though mine might be the billion-and-second).

Everybody's talking about the matter. Which means (of course!) that everyone cares.

Thanks again, Roger. You're doing a marvelous job. (And there'll be a little something extra in your next paycheck. [wink])

PART TWELVE
A ROSE BY ANY OTHER NAME...

And now the name controversy – even though the first Commish was none other than Jim Thorpe, the Native American Olympian turned football player, many teams have had names related to Native Americans.

The term Redskins is said by many pundits to be "derogatory to Native Americans" but then cannot produce said Native Americans torqued by the name.

There are schools on Native American lands in the western United States who also use the nickname "Redskins" for their team... and they *are* those people, of that supposed skin coloration... if you catch my drift.

Still the Washington Redskins has a long and less-than-glorious history of racism. George Preston Marshall absolutely refused to integrate his team. Whites only was his rule. It took the direct orders of President John F. Kennedy to get him to finally bring in some black players.

Yes, Kennedy was a big fan of the game, you'll recall.

Snyder's Last Stand

Dan Snyder, the team's owner, has fought hard against all the dark forces of evil who have tried to get him to change the name of his team.

He flat out refuses. He will not budge.

Even in the face of continued ridicule... People saying it should be changed to the Redfaces, the Redskin Potatoes, the Washington Braves, the Washington Natives, or the Washington Twenty-Ninth Amendments or some such.

Even though the patent office has removed his legal hold on the name and emblem of the team, he still will not budge.

The suspension of his rights to the name is really quite meaningless. Even though the patent and trademark no longer stands, the rights to the image is still upheld by the NFL and their marvelous legal staff will prosecute any infringement to the fullest extent of the law.

No, you really don't want to go there, believe me.

Look what Roger's legal beagles did after deflategate.

That sucker may be going to the Supreme Court, fer chrissakes!

Yes, these fellows take their legal rights very seriously.

The Cavalry is Coming

The use of the name has not really impacted anyone. Not here, not in the fandom, not in the hallowed halls of justice or anywhere else.

Although I must say that dandy Dan has gotten more cozy with several different tribes around the country to improve his image at not just owning *the* Redskins but for also owning… or at least supporting some of the native tribes.

They might be able to keep this sponsor with deep-pockets in their corner for some time to come if the pressure keeps up. As much as Snyder rarely seems to do anything altruistic, this may come as close as the fellow will ever get.

If some of his fortune goes to benefit the tribes out west, I am all for it. Having grown up in Arizona for a while, I know they can use all the help they can get.

All Apples and Oranges

There was a recent controversy over a certain state flying the Confederate Flag. Many people have jumped on the bandwagon and quite a few of the articles I have read show a vast chasm between public perception and truth.

Since most aspects of that "ominous" controversy don't really apply, I won't touch on it here except to wonder why many current pundits are now equating the use of the Confederate battle flag with the use of the name "Redskins".

If they were referring to the curious point of history that the Confederate States of America had peaceful treaties with many of the Native American tribes, unlike the purer race north of the Mason-Dixon line. Or that many of the Native Americans fought alongside their allies against the Union troops…

Other than that I cannot make out what the correlation is supposed to be about.

PART THIRTEEN
FOOTBALL CONSPIRACY THEORY

One might note that Walter Camp, that Yale athlete who is called "the father of football" was a member of the Skull and Bones group at Yale and this brings to mind the dark shadows of conspiracy. Well, at least to the minds of conspiracy theorists, Skull and Bones is an ominous group. Most people heard of the group while Bush II was President and the group was supposed to take on some very sinister characteristics over time.

And the conspiracy talk does not simply end there, either.

President Kennedy was quite fond of football, frequently playing the game with his family at weekends and trips back to Hyannis Port, as well as making sure he attended the annual Army-Navy game. He naturally rooted for Navy.

He was planning to attend the Army-Navy game in Chicago in early November 1963 when a plot was discovered. Kennedy did not make the journey but probably because of the assassination of the leader of South Vietnam rather than word on any danger from Chicago.

Of course, later that same month he traveled to Dallas and we all know what happened there.

Two of the wealthy oilmen in Dallas have frequently been mentioned in ominous, hushed undertones as co-conspirators. H. L. Hunt and Clint Murchison had no connection to the sport under examination but both of them had sons who *were*.

Lamar Hunt (son of H. L. Hunt) formed the Dallas Texans of the AFL and Clint Murchison Jr. formed the Dallas Cowboys of the NFL. And since Texas was not big enough for the two of them, Lamar took his team north where they became the Kansas City Chiefs.

So, in several respects, the sport and the Kennedy assassination are connected.

What that has to do with anything, however, I cannot quite grasp. But then, I'm not a conspiracy theorist.

I am certain – if Goodell was a conspiracy theorist – the Commish could easily show us how the above was linked to the assassination... but somehow wound through the underbelly of the Patriot organization. Roger, like many other fans, would simply love to see Brady and Belichick nailed for *something*, right?

Profiling

For the most part, the owners of the teams generally keep a low profile. They should allow their teams to be the newsmakers, not themselves.

Most people do not know that the original owners of the two Texas football teams – the Dallas Cowboys and the Dallas Texans (of the AFL) – were the sons of rich oilmen whom many conspiracy theorists have saddled with the assassination of President Kennedy.

And while it may be thought that would be reason enough to keep a low profile, the truth is these gentlemen already had a low profile even before that horrific event. Murchison kept the Cowboys until he died and the next owner has been the opposite sort of owner, a new breed so to speak, the sort of owner where Snyder might feel right at home.

Lamar Hunt, owner of the Texans moved his team to Kansas City where the name "Texans" would sound a bit foolish and it was changed the "The Chiefs". And they were winning championships long before the Cowboys did. But, of course, they were simply AFL championships. No big deal, apparently. At least until Broadway Joe Namath came to present the winds of change.

Still, I don't think anyone ever tried to point the bloody Kennedy finger in their direction. After all, the teams were already a reality *before* Kennedy became President and I don't recall any sort of interest from the Executive in the football going's on in Texas.

He was kept more than a bit busy applying pressure to the owner of the Redskins.

Other Mysteries

There seem to be a lot of stories about strange doings and dealings in the NFL. Most of them, however, lead nowhere.

After O. J. Simpson retired from football, he had a bit of an altercation that wound up in court. I'm sure you heard something about that.

At the time there were some people trying to relate his actions – somehow – to the sport of football. Maybe they were looking around for some medical reasons for his act… perhaps related to concussions or something.

We know that several players have come to a messy end over probable injury-related issues. Junior Seau was plagued by depression related to repeated head injuries and took his own life.

Many other players have had ailments that led to an early demise as well.

The League, of course, utilize their massive-retainered legal team to keep the taint away from their doorstep.

Studies done have led to lawsuits, and those have led to rule changes to make the game safer for all concerned. It's a good thing, too, as most of us want to see our favorite players continue to play for many years to come.

Well, all except for that demon incarnate, Tom Brady.

Has anyone else ever noticed that he does not seem to age…?

(That's a joke, of course.)

UnConspiracy Theory

Every year, it seems, there is some fan somewhere who comes up with a small conspiracy theory on why their team did so poorly.

Usually, of course, it is the refs who seem to be against their guys. If not the refs, then the league offices, or something. Sometimes – very rarely – someone hints that the team owner is somehow rigging the team to lose for some bizarre nefarious reason.

Personally, I don't think there is anything going on of that sort in the NFL. We have the occasional bad reffing call, the more frequent erroneous game plan or defensive scheme fiasco, but most of the conspiracies are on a much smaller scale.

Getting rid of Tebow was such an action but it wasn't much of a conspiracy. John Elway simply showed his disgust for the fellow and had him traded. Even if Peyton had not been their new go-to guy, Tebow was going to be history. There was no surprise in any of that.

Likewise, Rex Ryan's misuse/lack of use of Tebow was pretty much the same. No matter how much the team offices wanted Tebow, he didn't and wasn't going to make use of the guy.

The same way Gregg Williams marginalized the best defensive player on the Redskins.

These are not the stuff of conspiracy theory. No, this is outright stupidity and small-mindedness in action. It is just some people who cannot seem to see the big picture.

Sometimes it works out okay, like Denver got to the Super Bowl twice with Peyton though they now have a mess getting a QB to fill those shoes.

And Williams is at another team and doing okay, it seems.

Who knows what the future may bring?

Probably not a conspiracy.

PART FOURTEEN
ALIENS IN THE NFL

No, I'm not talking about illegal aliens or those players from foreign countries (I'll let Donald Trump use that stuff for his campaign), I'm talking the *real* E.T. thing. I haven't heard this theory bandied about for quite a few years (thank goodness!) but I thought I would resurrect it here. If aliens were going to invade, what better venue than through football, huh? Imagine the team wins the SB and – on live TV no less – they hoist the Lombardi trophy and unmask as extraterrestrials.

We would be at their mercies once they have hijacked the game. We would have no choice, would we?

The strangest playoff game

This thing here has just GOT TO BE about aliens, right?

The strangest playoff game of last season was Green Bay at Seattle.

Certainly Seattle's defense was fairly good in keeping Green Bay out of the end zone but the field goals were really stacking up.

Fourth quarter five-and-a-half minutes to play, Green Bay's Burnett intercepted a Wilson pass and quickly dropped to the turf.

I was like WTF?? Troy Aikman praised the guy for going down and I thought what sort of weird football universe was I in? There was still way too much time on the clock!

Then the Green Bay came in and ran the ball three times to "run down the clock".

I could understand them doing this if there was only a buck-forty on the clock but they were giving the Seahawks the ball back with something like a week to play. Hadn't these guys ever looked at any films of Wilson play?

Seattle got a touchdown and then the Burnett drop was assisted by another drop on the on-sides kick and it was game over.

Most analysts are yapping about the onside kick fiasco but none of that would have happened if Rodgers had come out with pretty good field position and played to win, not just run out the clock.

What was Mike McCarthy thinking?

These coaches just drive me completely nucking futs!

I figure it could only have been some sort of alien mind control.

He, Robot

There was a Twilight Zone I saw many years ago – somewhere back in the shadowy mists of history when baseball was still "America's game" – and this fellow had built a robot that could pretty much hit a homerun every time at bat.

By the end of the episode, of course, the robot had malfunctioned and the team went under. Though a new team started up that had a weirdly perfect pitching crew.

SciFi, we love you, but it isn't real in the sports world.

However, I read one commenter many years ago professing a theory that Tom Brady was a robot, or an alien. He said the fellow was too good, too perfect.

To Belichick's list of "crimes" we can now add: *posing a robot as a player*.

I don't think so.

This is just a case where all the many hours of practice, practice, practice have paid off. He is supposed to use the same mechanics with every pass. It's not science fiction, it's practice.

No, he's not a robot… but I'm not ruling out the alien angle just yet.

A Little Scary?

Brady almost pulled off the perfect season for the Patriots a few years ago by going 16-0 during the regular season. The nemesis that year was not Peyton but the other Manning brother whose Giants ended the New England run for perfection.

A couple of years ago, New England faced the defending SB champion Seattle Seahawks and prevented Russell Wilson's back-to-back wins by a last minute interception at the goal line to seal the win as Brady ran out the clock.

People wondered how Pete Carroll could have blown such a call… after all the Meast had run the ball so well up to that point that another handoff should have given them the touchdown and the win. More alien mind-control?

Personally, I thought his call was brilliant.

The last few runs had been gaining less and less yardage each time. It is almost as if New England (along with 99.9% of the viewing audience) was reading the Seahawks' minds. If the run was stopped again, it would be over anyway.

Everyone expected a run. Which was the best reason in the world to *not* run. It didn't work so well but Carroll knew they might be in trouble anyway.

The first half had ended with them scoring and giving the Patriots only 24 seconds to the half. Brady. Scored. Anyway.

Now, here at the end of the game, they were going to give Brady another minute to work with even had they scored a touchdown.

I thought Carroll did the best he could in the face of such odds.

Too bad it didn't work.

Bizarro World

Yes, that Super Bowl was a little strange at the end but the previous year's SB – the one Seattle won – started really bizarre.

Most people raved about Denver (well, Peyton, of course) being the highest scoring offense in the league and how they were going to beat up on the league's best defense, Seattle.

However, most analysts seem to have forgotten the old adage that "defense wins the big games", meaning the playoffs.

But Seattle's defense had a little help.

After the opening kickoff, Denver started the game by centering the ball a little too high and wide for Peyton and he had to chase the ball back into the endzone for a safety.

Not a pretty sight.
And the game went downhill from there.
It was almost as if someone had jinxed the Broncos.
Someone even suggested a passing UFO.
But I don't think so.

In SB 50, many were wondering if a similar fate would befall Peyton and the Broncos and 27 out of 28 NFL.com analysts predicted the winner would be the Carolina Panthers, the #1 offense for the season.

Are these guys aliens, or what?

We saw the same thing in SB XLVIII (48 for those Roman numerically challenged) except then the Broncos were the #1 offense. In SB 50 they returned as the #1 **defense**.

However, most analysts seem to have forgotten the old adage that "defense wins the big games", meaning the playoffs, as I said before.

And, once again, the #1 defense beat the #1 offense.

No jinx, no voodoo, no aliens, and the game was a lot closer than the previous one where Peyton lost.

Thank goodness.

Unbalanced Universes

Most of the Super Bowl games – and I have, so far, watched fifty of the things – seem extremely unbalanced. The scores are usually a little lopsided a disproportionate amount of the time.

The close nail-biters are the rarity.

It would almost seem like the coaches have put together a game plan (or scheme) that fails from the outset and they cannot adjust it well enough to dig themselves out of the hole once they are deep in it.

Since it IS the Big Game, I should imagine a lot of the players are a bit tense. Most of them will never make it back to this venue… they know it and it seems to rattle a lot of them.

Not science fiction, not aliens, not voodoo, just people being people-y.

CHAPTER FIFTEEN
MIRACLES AND MAYHEM

In the previous section, we examined the science fiction take on the NFL, now we take the scientific (& religious) view of the game.

As I mentioned above in the draft selection process, there are certain metrics the scouts, coaches and personnel evaluating people use to determine the best players.

You see, that's all about the science... the numbers. Probably the first coach who really got deep into this stuff was Tom Landry of the Cowboys. Yes, he was the first who brought computers into the mix to evaluate players and pop out the names of the best prospects.

But just as science cannot measure the immeasurable, the defining "it" that raises one certain player above the mediocre cannot be measured. It is some indefinable quality... some call it a knack, a gift, or such but it is definitely not something they include in the combine.

Otherwise Brady and Montana would have been taken in the first round.

And that brings us to Tim Tebow.

There was that joke that the televangelist mega-church preacher Joel Osteen had about Tebow. I don't suppose the Creator of the Universe still lives in a blue and orange dwelling anymore. Perhaps it awaits the color of the next team Tebow is destined for.

If any.

Does the Creator Have Favorites?

I have seen games and plays over the years that were miraculous. Heck, even the final last ditch pass in a close game is called the "Hail Mary". In the season just passed, Aaron Rodgers won two games late in the season with the Hail Mary.

Seems these guys still have a prayer of winning.

Reggie White – and others – would hold a small prayer service for their team on the sidelines before the game and more than one player in the league is a registered minister. There are a lot of players who talk their connection with the Divine on and off the field, in their play and in their normal lives.

And many players look upward and point to the heavens after making a score or cross themselves… or Tebow.

There are a vast number of players who talk quite openly about their faith and how having such deep faith has kept them going through all the hardships faced to get to where they are today.

I am not certain that the Creator actually has a favorite team… Many seem to think Satan favors the Patriots, but I don't know about that either. I suppose if the guys on both teams are praying to God, who is He gonna let win?

Maybe He just likes to watch the game unfold like the rest of us.

Perhaps a "Redskins curse"?

There is an unusual stat for the Redskins. Fortunately it is not a shoe-in but several QBs cut by the team went on to get a SB ring elsewhere.

Trent Green played in 1998 but was gone for 1999. In 2000 he won a SB ring on the St. Louis roster. A little strange, I suppose but not really that weird.

Then came Brad Johnson who had a really good year in 1999. 2000 wasn't so hot so they got rid of the fellow. 2001 he started for Tampa and in 2002 won a SB with that team.

The next few QBs were not so lucky but then we come to Mark Brunell. He was cut after the 2006 season and went to the Saints. In 2009 he got a SB ring with that team.

It did not seem to help Patrick Ramsey or Danny Wuerffel – son of a Lutheran minister – or several others cut by the team. And we'll have to wait and see about RG3… although for him to get the Browns to the SB would be nothing short of miraculous.

The current Redskins QB, Kirk Cousins, is also the son of a minister. Maybe he has an inside pipeline. We will have to wait and see.

Having already touched on the miracle that Tebow brought to Denver, let's see if the love spread anywhere else.

Trying, Dying to Take it Back

I saw a very interesting article at Huffington post where Jeff Darlington mentioned some reports in a New York paper by several teammates of Tebow who claim the reason he isn't playing instead of Sanchez is because the boy is simply "terrible"!

Darlington tweeted: "@JeffDarlington: Hey, Jets players who anonymously ripped Tim Tebow to the NY Daily News today... The Broncos of Aug 2011 called. They want their quotes back."

Yes, the Bronco fans were really pissed when Tebow arrived in Denver... they would have preferred a "good quarterback". And let's face it, Elway was very quick to send the boy up the river (the Hudson River, of course) at the end of the season.

But the fans might want to eat those words after they got to ride the Tebow train into the playoffs... and should we say after rolling over the Jets?... nah, let's play nice. Yes, the mediocre quarterback seemed to be a little bit better than anyone thought he could be.

But let's get realistic here. Mark Sanchez was taken high in the draft to be *the guy* in the Jets organization. And, yes, his early promise seems to have faded a little since then...

Well, maybe a LOT. After all, there are 31 other QB's in the league rated better. And that would place Sanchez at... hm, let me see... oh, yeah, dead last.

So I can understand why the fans are so upset that Rex Ryan ("he of the rather large mouth") won't use Tebow better. And I can understand why the "anonymous teammates" that threw Tebow under the bus want things to stay as they are:

If the quarterback was better – and who could *not* be better than Sanchez? – then the rest of the team would actually have to start performing at something closer to a semblance of a professional level which means they would have to get off their overpaid behinds and do the job the fans expect of them rather than telling those same fans to shut up.

Maybe they forgot who is really paying their salaries – in the long run – just like the ownership of the NFL or the commish himself.

It seems to be some sort of disease creeping through the league and it is spreading its infection everywhere, from the top down.

I don't know... maybe we should pray on it.

Ready for a little Tebowing?

What Is It With the Jets?

Sure we know that everyone ♥ New York but is the place becoming the "vacation year" for athletes?

Brett Favre came out of retirement and Green Bay immediately shipped the guy off to the Jets for one year. Then he was traded to Minnesota the next year and took them on a pretty good run into the playoffs; one win away from the Super Bowl.

Then Tim Tebow went to the same Jets for – apparently – only one year before being shipped off to who knows where... probably Jacksonville, where he wanted to go in the first place rather than... well, New York, which everyone ♥, by the way.

I know there is not enough data here to make any decent statistical analyses but what is going on here? Is New York the new sabbatical, or is it more of the new "Time Out" corner for slightly bizarre players? (Sure, you want to add "and coaches"... but Ryan has been there for more than a year.)

Maybe it is just some sort of jinx. I mean, two rather exceptional (though much maligned) quarterbacks have both spent their year in purgatory (i.e. New York Jets organization, not the city, which everyone ♥'s) in utter mediocrity before moving on to another place, like where they wanted to go in the first place.

Do the Jets just not know how to use talent when they get it or what? I mean, they did pretty good back in the days of Broadway Joe. He was able to take them places...

Ah, but that was in the days before Broadway Rex.

Don't ya just ♥ New York?

Mile High Shocker

Peyton's first year in Denver and he, quite naturally, got them into the playoffs just like the maligned Tebow did the year before.

The Divisional Round of the playoffs turned out pretty much as anticipated with the home teams winning in all but one of the contests. And that one was a surprise.

All the analysts over at nfl.com had picked, unanimously, that the Broncos would have won that game. I guess nobody told the Ravens.

The reffing in the game was no better or worse than the other games I have seen this year except once again I had wished it would have been the replacement refs so the lousy calling could have been excused. But that is such a common gripe this season that is goes *almost* without saying, except to say it really sucked, as usual.

Still when we went to overtime, I was fully expecting that when the Broncos got their turn that Peyton was going to do the Tebow on the first play and catch Demaryius Thomas on a crossing route and the guy would take it to the house.

Unfortunately, the play calling went for the safe and utterly predictable run, which netted a yard, because it was what the Ravens had anticipated.

Things went downhill rapidly from there.

They should have Tebowed.

And they would be playing next week.

Tebow's brother had a few choice tweets about the inability of the Broncos effectiveness in the O.T. Period.

He said it was John Elway's karma and that the record still stands that the last QB to win a playoff game in Denver was the QB that is not supposed to be a very good, or at least not and NFL-caliber QB, Tim Tebow.

You know, NFL-caliber, like... well, Peyton Manning.

Regardless, Peyton has been in the playoffs practically every year he has played, so I expected him to be back.

Like we are so used to saying here in Redskins country, "there's always next year".

Peyton did, of course, get back to the playoffs the next year but lost the Super Bowl. Two years later, he won SB 50 and retired. And Tebow is still looking for a team...

I'm Just Sayin'...

While it is a truism that no good deed goes unpunished, and equally true that sometimes you've only got one shot...
It is also true that a man is greater than the sum of his parts.
The new GM for the Jacksonville Jaguars – the team everyone assumed Tebow would next play for – has announced they really have no place in their organization for the man.
Most people have said that Tebow did miserably while at the Jets... but when was he given the chance? They used him sparingly over the season. The "brilliant" (a self-proclaimed moniker, I believe) coach Ryan would rather lose with Sanchez.
Tebow's brother tweeted his side of the argument but he has no say in the matter. (If you missed that, he basically reminded everyone that the last playoff win in Denver was by none other than his brother, Tim.)
Analysts all claim that both Denver and New York have said he is a "terrible" QB.
If Tebow was such a bad QB, how could he take Denver on such a wild ride into the playoffs? Probably, had he gone all the way to the Super Bowl, they would still have said the same thing.
Why?
Because in practice, Tebow looks lousy.
Therefore he cannot play good enough for the NFL, right?
But practice is not the same as the game and some people are simply better when put in the right conditions.
A fine example of that is Kaepernick, the young QB who rallied the 49ers to beat the Packers, and that's after he threw a pick-six on the opening drive.
Picking talent is a seemingly rare talent. There are too many stories about the "draft busts" over the years. Choices made by people *supposedly* good at judging talent.

Yet, as many people know, it is not always the quality of the stars that means the most. I remember a certain team out of Miami that was not full of the greatest stars in the NFL but they seem to have gone undefeated. Later greats like Dan Marino could not surround himself with a *team* like that.

What is that indefinable thing that causes some people to form into a great team, and for the individual parts to become better than they otherwise might have been?

Joe Montana was picked in the third round because they said he did not have arm strength that was NFL caliber. They said he couldn't compete in the NFL.

Tom Brady was chosen in the sixth round because he looked positively horrible at the Combine. They said he couldn't compete in the NFL.

And that shows you what their statistics and miles of "practice" footage will get you.

Tebow deserves a shot because he has *already* shown he can do the job.

But I don't think anyone in the NFL is smart enough to know it. Or to look back at *that* footage.

a Tale of Two... uh, Tales

Breaking ESPN News: *Tim Tebow Was Forced on New York Jets Owner Woody Johnson, GM Candidate Interviewee says.*

I saw this story posted under some video with "sports commentator" (and I use the term lightly) Skip Bayless pontificating on the state of ... well, whatever it was he thought was important in that moment... I do not find him important enough to bother listening to anything he has to say...

But, this post is not about the Skipless, nor will I allow the Baylness to hijack this post, either. For this is about Two Cities: New York and – you guessed it! – New York.

The city so huge they had to name it twice. So huge that it actually has two pro football teams! And so huge that they cannot fit either of those teams actually in New York, so they outsource both to New Jersey.

Anyway, making a short story longer, the owner of the Jets was supposed to have been the one that was so hot to get Tebow, so adamant that he went after the fellow doggedly... and now it seems it was "forced" on him by an employee. Now what sort of inverted organization is that where an underling forces the boss to do anything?

And, apparently, Woody Johnson only recently made this discovery and fired the man who forced this travesty on the poor unsuspecting owner!! Shame on you GM Mike Tannenbaum!

And this shameless Tannenbaum even "forced" it on the President of the team as well. Either the owner and President were asleep for an awful long time or they bided their time to see if the former GM needed to be scapegoated. (Which, I believe, is one step less in severity than waterboarding... uh, whatever that is, huh?)

Let's face it, if Tannenbaum's little idea had taken the team to the Super Bowl, they would have announced that it had been the owner's idea and he was a freakin' genius!

But we can leave that parallel universe/alternate history for the fiction accounts sure to be released at the next ComicCon or IguanaCon, or what-have-you. We will deal with the facts here.

Tebow, a veritable force to be reckoned with, was forced on the unsuspecting Big Apple, after becoming the much hailed "last Denver QB to win a playoff game" – and the record still stands these many months later – to become the backup to future hall-of-famer [*maybe*, you never know… Hey, it *could* happen!] Mark Sanchez, well known for his famous "playing dead" posturing on the field so he doesn't have to actually tackle anyone, or pass, or run, or – you know – win games and for the patented "butt fumble".

May-the-forced-Tebow-be-with-you did not sit well with the omnipresent Coach Ryan and he could not figure out how to use the clutch Heisman trophy player since he assumed they already had what he unhesitatingly called "a quarterback". The man needs more than just his eyesight examined.

So they stood Tebow on the sidelines most of the season waiting for someone to cast the first stone... making sure none of the aforementioned objects flew in the direction of Coach Ryan who was... as you can guess... blameless! Because... as you can probably guess... Tebow had been forced on him!!!

Stoic Tebow did all the menial chores he was assigned, waiting patiently for the powers that be to notice Sanchez was a complete loser and sit the boy down and send in a real QB. You know, one who had taken his team to the playoffs and won a postseason game. But Ryan – again without the use of anything resembling good eyesight – misread his depth charts and sent in the wrong backup, forgetting the listed backup QB, Tebow, even existed... And I have heard rumors that the coach is actually on medication so he can do just that: forget Tebow exists.

Now the truth will out and it seems no one in the Big Apple actually wanted Tebow in the first place... Who knows who forced the idea on Tannenbaum!! So he was forced onto a team that nobody wanted, except for the *fourteen gazillion fans who finally anticipated a playoff berth under the guidance of said same Tebow.*

And that's the tale of two cities: New York (Jekyll) and New York (Hyde). The first has a Manning – not the one who isn't the last QB to win a playoff game in Denver [if that phrase even makes sense!] – and the second has no QB, no management, no coaching, no responsibility, and no hope of any future. For the moment, at least.

The End.

I hope you enjoyed my little tale.

Personally, I am tired of the Tebow bashers and Tebow haters. I say give the guy a freakin' chance before you bust his chops.

He surprised even his toughest critics in Denver by stepping in and turning their 2011 season around, getting into the playoffs and beating a team who was supposed to roll over them easily enough. Sure, Tebow didn't make it all the way to the Super Bowl but there were 30 other teams who didn't make it either. Cut him a little slack, fer chrissakes!

And people say he was a loser in NY. But when did the guy ever get the chance to show us what he has. Punt blocking? You'd think Tom Brady was a lousy player too if he only came in to punt block and run the wildcat on tough third down situations when everyone (yes, even the opposing teams) knew that Brady was going to get the ball.

They would not do that to Brady, or Manning (either of them), Flacco, Roethlisberger, Kaepernick, or any other QB in the NFL who has already **proven** his ability to win games. No, not even Sanchez, whose production is still more than a little iffy in that department. Even Romo does not have to punt block or that other stuff.

Blame Ryan, Tannenbaum, Johnson, his Woody, or even Skip Bayless, but stop blaming Tebow for having a lousy year in New York. They never gave him a shot.

Of course, loyal Jets fans will be back next season, regardless of the outcome of this fiasco. That's what the fans do.

Many were certain Rex Ryan would give them an even bigger and better fiasco the next season. That's what *he* does. We're still waiting for him to really shine in Buffalo.

Another Missionary Moment Gone South

Tim Tebow was scheduled to speak at the mega-First Baptist Church of Dallas but has canceled his April appearance there.

Many people were upset because the pastor of the church, Robert Jeffress, is supposedly outspoken on the subject of gays, same-sex marriage, idolaters, Muslims, Mormons, Catholics... well, I think you get the idea. Everything that is *not* a First Baptist or Jesus is under fire.

So, what's the fuss? Most preachers I know – Baptist, Methodist, Lutheran, Anglican, Presbyterian, what-have-you – are a little outspoken on the same subjects. I think that sort of goes hand-in-hand with the religion they are touting.

Of course, modern Christians who believe more in what Jesus was preaching – forgiveness, not casting the first stone, universal love and peace... you know, that namby-pamby side of the Savior – don't have a problem with any of this.

And supposedly, neither did Tim Tebow. That is, until the furor started.

Now the gay-press is applauding his sensibilities while the Christian press is dragging his image over hot coals... yes, just like Jesus did, right? I mean that *is* somewhere in the scriptures, isn't it?

And I have read two separate articles that mention "Tebow's handlers"... Jeffress himself appeared on a radio show and said "I believe as long as he listens to the Holy Spirit and to God's voice and maybe not that of his handlers, you know, I think he will stand firm, and we're counting him to do that."

I was not aware that young men of his stature required "handlers".

But let's get one thing straight: Tebow *is* religious and he has spoken in churches before and will, no doubt, continue that practice. It is his *ministry*. And Christianity is the religion he is ministering in. Even to those who do not precisely share the views of Jesus, or Tebow, or the Gay Rights movement.

Somewhere along the way, the unyielding will drop the stone they *so* want to cast, their speech will become more tolerant, and everyone will learn how to live peaceably with one another...

Probably about the time the football season starts up again and we can get down to what's really important.

Beer nuts, anyone?

Quarterback Mania

The Jets were having QB competition according to their Head Coach, Rex Ryan. He seemed to have gotten over his personal "Mark Madness" and realized Sanchez may just not be their "go-to" guy.

Yes, Mark Sanchez, Greg McElroy, David Garrard, yes and even Tim Tebow, all got to compete for the role.

And as if that wasn't too many QB's the Jets were also looking to acquire Kevin Kolb, but he'd just signed with another New York team, Buffalo... yes, that's a football team, what'd you think it was?

So, they are making noise about wanting to draft Geno Smith as another QB.

And with five QB's on their roster, one can only wonder if it will be enough?

That's a joke, right?

Even working all five in rotation, I don't think they've got a prayer.

[Sorry, Tim]

a Real Song of Ice and Fire

On May 9th in 2015, Mike Florio reported that Mike Silver of Yahoo! Sports (a man of questionable authority to begin with) that "Belichick hates Tebow".

As if the story did not already have too many Mikes in the equation, they went on to quote "organizational sources" and "unnamed head coaches" to firm up the claim.

Six weeks ago, Tebow was released by the Jets to – as most assumed – fade away into obscurity. When I read the original Mike Florio article to my wife, I said it sounded like a bit of misdirection by the guys in Foxboro if it was actually really said by anyone attached to the Patriots organization.

If misdirection was intended, it worked like a charm and now all the commentators are proclaiming it was the "perfect match" all along.

Whatever.

The Jets may have taken Tebow originally with the idea of *doing something* with him but never quite figured out what that might be. What would one expect with Ryan running the team? He has trouble figuring which *side* of the donut to eat first.

The sports talking-heads are now saying that Belichick always likes taking on "projects" and many have not turned out well. Remember Albert Haynesworth?

But other ones have turned out pretty good, like Randy Moss.

And Belichick has a way of shutting down the "media circus" that seems to follow Tebow wherever he goes.

True, true, and true... but these guys are still overlooking one final thing that might be a more interesting angle:

Belichick loves to get the New York Jets' goat whenever he can. Whether spying on them or simply trashing them (not hard to do, it seems) Bill loves to goad the Jets.

Now he can – possibly – use a tool they discarded against them in a very public way.

I doubt he will pull Brady out of the games against the Jets (two a year, if memory serves me) but I can certainly see him using the fellow in the games to show them what they coulda, woulda, shoulda done.

Darren Sharper (an analyst at NFL network) contends that the entire thing is a mistake that Tebow is not a quarterback... apparently he has never seen any of the stats from his high school, collegiate, or NFL career. Either that or he simply tends to ignore the stats because "everyone knows" he can't play quarterback. I, among one at least, think that this NFL network analyst, Darren, should get a *little sharper* before he enlightens us with more of his marvelous opinions.

But Darren's attitude is a very Rex Ryan attitude to take. And we can see how well it served him and the Jets last year.

Many people think the Patriots are taking Tebow to change him into a tight end or running back. But, no, he has been hired as a quarterback.

If there can be any good brought from this relationship, you know Belichick will find it. Maybe not this season, but later on. Brady will not last forever. Not saying Tebow is his logical heir, but who knows what the future may bring.

The Wizard of Oz and the Wizard of Menlo Park are really no match for the man behind the curtain in Foxboro. The wizard in the gray hoodie makes the incomprehensible seem to make more sense that the power struggles behind each episode of "Game of Thrones".

So there will be no quarterback controversy in New England like we saw in Denver and New York. No one is going to doubt that Brady is **the** starting quarterback.

And there will no longer be a Tebow media circus... not in Foxboro. There, Belichick has always been the one-man circus.

Aaron, You Shoulda Listened to Tim

The Patriots cut Tebow at the end of the preseason, although Belichick had some very nice things to say about the guy. He did, however, keep Tebow's former college teammate, Aaron Hernandez.

Oops!

Even Belichick didn't see *this thing* coming!

Aaron Hernandez has been found guilty by a jury of his non-gansta peers and it seemed to come as a surprise to no one except Hernandez himself.

In the last few days, either he was "putting on an air of confidence" or he actually believed his high-priced lawyers were going to pull a rabbit out of a hat.

But Hernandez was no OJ, this perp had no juice. And though he was able to get rid of much of the incriminating evidence, the jury saw through the charade. Aaron's lost his mojo and will probably spend his life behind bars trying to make himself a kingpin in the prison population somewhere.

If he had paid more attention to his QB back at Florida... but then, Aaron was so little like his Biblical namesake and he probably thought Tebow a bit of a pansy with all that praying and stuff.

Tebow prayed, now Aaron pays.

Maybe he'll find God in prison... so many do.

Professional Football is Imploding in Florida

It was bad enough that Jacksonville refused to take the locally charmed Tim Tebow and earn the complete distrust and disgust of their fans by producing a less-than-lackluster team, the remainder of Florida seemed to have joined in the "Peninsula curse".

But I don't really think we can blame Tebow for any of this... can we? Unless the scriptures somewhere tell us that "the peninsula will be lost if one turns their back on the Man of God" or something like that.

Anyway, after Jacksonville buckled to the curse, Tampa Bay was beset with a scourge of virus and bacterial infestation... somewhat less than seven plagues, but you get the drift.

Some of their team have gotten very ill from the microbes and their coach (some say who has a brain the size of a microbe) is acting fairly odd in his decision making.

This mess might be entirely overlooked if either team had one win between them but they are – strangely enough – the *only* two teams in the NFL without a win this season! This has Biblical connotations *all over it*!!

Still, there was one bright spot in this fiasco: Miami is sitting at .500 (4 wins, 4 losses) and are not the bearers of the golden goose egg shared by the other two Florida franchises but now it seems they have a mess the size of Texas. And maybe a bigger mess than the other two teams combined.

It seems Jonathan Martin (no relation to Trayvon) has gone AWOL from the team amid swirling rumors of hazing, practical jokes, and other good-natured football camaraderie. Perhaps the fellow just has thin skin.

Then, the story took a turn to the South and it seems that one player named Ricky (whose name will remain Incognito) has been badgering the fellow for some time now (like since last year) and has been using racial slurs, threats, innuendo, and half a dozen other nuanced behaviors that I thought were beyond the mental capability of the one who shall remain Incognito.

It is a sad day for Miami, a sadder day for Florida, and an even bigger black day for the NFL. Oh, did I mention Jonathan Martin is black? (That might frame the story in a different light.)

So, what looked like a simple case of an emotionally frail young man not being able to take some friendly ribbing, it now seems his teammate has been involved in criminal behavior of a very bad sort.

And the rest of the team seems to have known something of this and did nothing about it.

Sure, New England had Hernandez and the murder-thing – so very easy to see that sort of thing and handle it – but this does not bode well for anyone.

If the league cannot get this sort of behavior under control (and there were shades a couple of weeks ago of the same sort of thing going on in Tampa) they are going to *wish* their only problems were a few concussion cases, illegal tackle fines, and the racial slur contained in the names of their teams.

Maybe everyone in Florida should take a moment and do a little Tebowing?

And perhaps Tim could bring some salvation.

Or at least a little salve.

Tebow Soaring? Not Just Yet

Last season, Philly signed Tim Tebow to a one year deal but that could have meant anything.

Other than reporter Trent Dilfer, every other commentator in the sports press seems to think it is going to be a waste of time, even though they all claim to have not yet gotten a chance to see the "new, improved Tebow". Most are still complaining over the "old Tebow" with most crowing the familiar refrain that you cannot change a leopard's spots. (Don't these guys realize the business they are in is called "news" and not "olds"?)

If they were correct in the idea that people cannot fundamentally change, I suppose Saul of Tarsus' tale of redemption on the road to Damascus was a lie. If people cannot change, I suppose Alcoholics Anonymous doesn't really help anyone set aside their addictions. And, it should also figure that every heartwarming story of redemption and forgiveness in the history of the world is nothing but a sham.

One thing *I know does not change* is these people's attitude about Tebow.

I am hoping that Chip Kelly can prove all these people wrong by pulling off one of the great coaching miracles he has been known for.

And it won't even matter if the talking heads praise Tim's success as proof of Kelly's brilliance rather than his abilities.

Which, of course, is how they will slant the story. Cannot admit they could have been wrong, y'know.

A Tale of Redemption Re-Placed on Hold

Tebow was released by Chip Kelly and the Eagles organization and it doesn't look like anyone is rushing in to offer the guy another chance.

Like I have mentioned repeatedly in this tale of woe, no one can see past the numbers, even when the numbers show the guy can win.

They would rather stick with QBs with proven mediocrity than pick up a guy who might just improve their team's chances. Standard, par for the course, and more than just a little bit NFL lite.

Still, we have a plethora of teams to watch – with or without Tebow – and another bunch of losers set up for yet another season.

A Little NFL "Magic"

I remember when 9/11 happened back in 2001. All the games for that weekend were canceled. I was so disappointed because I needed something to bring me out of the funk from repeated viewings of the tragedy.

The League apparently thought it would be crass to play the games in light of what had happened.

It wasn't until a couple of years later that some bright boy at the NFL offices admitted that it would have helped the country heal by distracting us from the pain as well as bringing back a "sense of normalcy" into a world that had definitely gone a little pear-shaped.

Too little too late, my grandpa used to say.

PART SIXTEEN
SETTING YOUR SIGHTS A LITTLE LOWER

With the start of every season, the fan-base of each individual team in the NFL crosses their fingers and collectively prays for the hand of luck to be on them this year. Yes, these people have the faith of a Tebow that miracles can and do occur on this earthly plane in spite of what the numbers may say.

Even the teams who have been at the bottom (or very close to it) for several years, can dream that the football gods will turn the light in their direction. Even though the analysts place the evil eye on them – figuratively – they can still dream.

At least until after the first four games or so.

Once it becomes obvious the Big Game is not to be allotted to their team this year, they can still pull for a possible run at the playoffs. Some seek only the redemption of a winning season.

Others, not glimpsing even those glimmers, hope that their team can at least be a spoiler this year… possibly even knock some team they really hate out of the playoffs.

Some bitterly turn to the ranks of the college gridiron to start planning who they can draft next year to remove the blight from their team.

All Isn't Completely Filled With Darkness

Time sure flies when you're having fun… and sometimes it flies when you're not enjoying yourself as well.

The last championship won by the Cardinals was in 1947. Most of the teams in the league currently did not even exist at that time. The length of their championship drought is really quite amazing. And their fans have a good reason to feel disgruntled.

It has been over two decades since Washington brought home a Lombardi. Twelve different teams have achieved that goal more recently. That means there are **nineteen** teams in worse shape than the Redskins. And six of those have *never* won the Lombardi!

Yeah, yeah, I know. It does not make the Washington fans feel even the slightest better about their plight. It probably doesn't help any other team's fans either.

TEAM	YRS From Creation to First Championship	YRS Since Last Championship	TEAM
Cleveland Browns	0	0	Denver Broncos
Tennessee Titans	0	1	New England Patriots
Kansas City Chiefs	2	2	Seattle Seahawks
New York Giants	2	3	Baltimore Ravens
Chicago Bears	2	4	New York Giants
San Diego Chargers	3	5	Green Bay Packers
Buffalo Bills	4	6	New Orleans Saints
Baltimore Ravens	4	9	Pittsburgh Steelers
Indianapolis Colts	5	13	Indianapolis Colts
Washington Redskins	5	16	Tampa Bay Buccaneers
Detroit Lions	5	17	St. Louis Rams
Miami Dolphins	6	20	Dallas Cowboys
New York Jets	8	24	San Francisco 49ers
St. Louis Rams	9	29	Washington Redskins
Green Bay Packers	10	30	Chicago Bears
Carolina Panthers*	10+	31	Oakland Raiders
Dallas Cowboys	11	41	Miami Dolphins
Houston Texans*	13+	46	Kansas City Chiefs
Philadelphia Eagles	15	47	New York Jets
Oakland Raiders	16	50	Buffalo Bills
Seattle Seahawks	18	51	Cleveland Browns
Jacksonville Jaguars*	20+	52	San Diego Chargers
Tampa Bay Buccaneers	26	54	Tennessee Titans
Arizona Cardinals	27	55	Philadelphia Eagles
San Francisco 49ers	35	58	Detroit Lions
Denver Broncos	37	68	Arizona Cardinals
New England Patriots	41	N/A	Cincinnati Bengals
Pittsburgh Steelers	41	N/A	Houston Texans
New Orleans Saints	42	N/A	Jacksonville Jaguars
Cincinnati Bengals*	47+	N/A	Minnesota Vikings
Atlanta Falcons*	49+	N/A	Atlanta Falcons
Minnesota Vikings**	54+	N/A	Carolina Panthers

* – teams without a championship win
** – Minnesota won the NFL Championship game but then lost in Super Bowl IV, the final intra league contest as the two leagues merged thereafter. Most record books give them the NFL title but stipulate they did not win the *real* championship.

Oh, the Pain!

When last season got underway, there are a great number of Redskins fans – we were assured it is not a majority – were hoping the team will lose.

Yes, you heard that correctly: Redskins fans were hoping the team will lose. Seems they were fed up with the missteps over the RG3 situation and the obvious dysfunctionality of the franchise management.

They feel that if the team fell flat for another season, it would become obvious even to people like Dan Snyder that something is very rotten in the State of Redskins.

Many of those fans were hoping RG3 would resurrect the glory of his rookie year but other fans were even done with that guy. They wanted only to tear the club down and rebuild it with a new coach and some of next year's' draft prospects. Now with RG3 having been shown the door, the fans are thinking the team can focus on something different this year.

Personally, I don't think it matters if Snyder tears it down and starts over again next year, if he operates with his same philosophy moving forward we will see the insanity continue year after year after year.

So far, Jay Gruden is a joke. He demands respect when he has earned none and expects us to "understand" how he has had to deal with a troublesome situation.

After claiming for several months that there was no QB controversy and then changing horses so soon in the preseason tells the truer story: the man lied to all of us.

Sure, he can claim that it was business and merely saying what was politically correct at the time, but to put RG3 in harm's way in a preseason game like he did was much worse than a coaching error. It seems more of a premeditated hatchet job. Not only do I consider Gruden to be a classless coach, it does not speak well of him as a human being.

That sort of person does not *deserve* respect.

So, yeah, I am with the fans who want to see the fellow shown the exit. I am certain he will go on to some other team, and then maybe another team until luck works out for him and he does actually happen onto a good team.

A Tale of Redemption Re-Placed on Hold

Rather than hoping for a Lombardi every year, perhaps the best we can hope for is to see some really good football – even if inconsistent – for our team. Perhaps it will usher in a bit of stability even if only by showing how bad the leadership of the current team is and pave the way for better leadership in the coming seasons.

Given a new situation might find the players capable of digging deep within themselves and becoming really the best they can be.

Perhaps it will only take a couple of wins to put them on the right track.

Or perhaps one of the players will step up and become a team leader.

One never knows in this sport since the league has tried to reach parity where any given team can beat any other given team on any given Sunday (or Thursday or Monday). The magic can be just around the corner, one incident away from the path to greatness.

Every player in the league wants to get to the Big Game. They each want to win every week or at least give it their best. The players are really the heart and soul of the game, not the coaches, not the owners, not the league.

The players want to please their fan-base.

And for all the blather and trash talk we have seen and heard over the years, for the most part each and every player does not view the other team as an enemy but rather another group of professionals attempting to do their best.

A game I saw in 2011 gave an image that struck me deeply. As is usual when a player is injured during a game, players from both sides generally gravitate onto the field to assist the fallen player anyway they can. They tend to stay out of the way of the trainers and doctors tending to the fellow but the players gather around in a show of support that says they are all truly brothers in this quest for perfection.

The announcers did not mention this, nor have I heard anyone else speak of this but the players formed a ring around the fallen comrade... and the shape was almost that of a well-known figure:

It most resembles a heart.

In Closing...

Now as we get ready to get underway with a new season, we've heard the hype from our head coach and the team leaders and – while trying to squelch the little doubts within about the players who just don't quite seem ready for that "breakaway season" – we are actually very hopeful for this season. With a little luck... Hey! There is always that, huh?

With a little luck and a fortunate bounce or two (or two hundred) we might actually be able to root our team into the playoffs and then: The BIG Game.

As the weeks progress, the more faint-hearted of us may grumble, gnash our teeth and shake our fists at the football gods, but the optimists among us can look at the silver lining: we might get the chance to be a spoiler and knock off some team we really hate, like the Cowboys, the Seahawks, or any team containing Tom Brady or that cheater Bill Belichick.

Win or lose, I still love football and I will continue to root for the home team no matter how miserable they play. And I will still root for those players not on my team that I love to watch every week around the league.

And this takes into account any and all machinations by the league offices, the umpires, the coaching staffs, and so forth. The excitement of the contest always overshadows any of the negative chatter about the game or its personnel.

Dissections of the games will continue around the water coolers – or on social media – the "what if's" will continue to be stated and the hopes and plans for the upcoming game will be discussed at length.

All this palaver will be for one purpose only, if truth be told.

We do this in order to stave off that inevitable, but horrible, conclusion of another season which will usher in the dreaded era known as "off-season".

Sure, the NFL throws us a few bones in the shape of Draft Day and perhaps another juicy scandal or two but nothing therein can replace the excitement of the games.

With a wink and a firm thumbs up, we can turn to like-minded optimistic fans and say, "This year may be a wash out but just wait until next year!"

The phrase itself offers hope. And that is really all we need.

APPENDIX

I do not mention all the quarterbacks who were drafted or who played in this era as many were completely unmemorable.

During this era, there are only six quarterbacks to enter the Hall of Fame without a Super Bowl win: Sonny Jurgensen, Fran Tarkenton, Dan Fouts, Warren Moon (undrafted), Jim Kelly, and Dan Marino.

Of the retired quarterbacks who have won a Super Bowl but never entered the HOF: the late Kenny Stabler, Jim Plunkett (two Super Bowl wins, the only such in the list), Joe Theismann, Jim McMahon, Phil Simms, Doug Williams, Jeff Hostetler, Mark Rypien, Trent Dilfer, and Brad Johnson. All the remainder are either still playing or are not yet eligible.

In the charts below, I have highlighted each draft which included a quarterback named to the Pro Bowl or the Hall of Fame. Those quarterbacks have been named. As you can see, there were a lot of quarterbacks drafted who did not do so well in the professional ranks. Quite a few of them had exceptional careers at the college level but seemed unable to translate to the professional game.

YEAR	16th	17th	18th	19th	20th	21st	22nd	23rd	24th	25th	26th	27th	28th	29th	30th
1955		1					1								
1956	2	3** **Bart Starr	1					1	1			1	1		1
1957		2		1		1	2						3		
1958					1										
1959			1* *Joe Kapp			1		1		1					
1960	1				1										
1961		1		1	2										
1962			4	1	1										
1963				1											
1964	1		1		4										
1965	1	1	1	1											
1966	1	2	1	1											

132

QUARTERBACKS DRAFTED

YEAR	1st	2nd	3rd	4th	5th	6th	7th	8th	9th	10th	11th	12th	13th	14th	15th
1955	2								1*				1		
									*Johnny Unitas						
1956	2*		1	1								1			
	*Earl Morrall														
1957	2*	1	1	2**	1		1				1	1			
	*John Brodie & Len Dawson **Sonny Jurgensen														
1958	1			2	2*					1		1	2		
					*Frank Ryan										
1959	4*	2**		1		undrafted - Tom Flores	1	1				1			
	*Dave Baker **Richie Petitbon														
1960	2	1	2*	1	1	1	1		1**			2			
			*Don Meredith						**Charley Johnson						
1961	2*		3**	1		1	1	1				3	1		
	*Norm Snead & Billy Kilmer **Fran Tarkenton														
1962	1*	2	1	1			1	2	1						
	*Roman Gabriel														
1963	1			1		1		1		3			1		
1964	2	2				2	1	2		2*	1**		1		
										*Roger Staubach	**Bob Berry				
1965	2*		1	1		1	1	1	1			1**		1	
	*Joe Namath & Craig Morton											**Ernie Kellerman			
1966	1			1		1	1	1			1		1		
	undrafted - Jim Hart														

YEAR	16th	17th	18th	19th	20th	21st	22nd	23rd	24th	25th	26th	27th	28th	29th	30th
1967	2	3													
1968	1	1													
1969	1	1													
1970	1														
1971															
1972	4	1													
1973		3													
1974		1													
1975		2													
1976		3													
1977															
1978															

QUARTERBACKS DRAFTED

YEAR	1st	2nd	3rd	4th	5th	6th	7th	8th	9th	10th	11th	12th	13th	14th	15th
1967	3*	1	1			4	2	1		1	1	1			
	*Bob Griese & Steve Spurrier														
1968	2*	3**	2		1	2	1	1			2	1	1	1	2
	*Greg Landry **Ken Stabler			undrafted - Sam Wyche											
1969	2	3			1			2*	1	2	2	2	1		
	(1st pick of draft was O J Simpson)							*James Harris							
1970	2*	2			1	3	1	2**				1			
	*Terry Bradshaw							**Mike Holmgren, famous coach of SF, GB, & Seattle							
1971	3*		4**	1***	1	2	1	1		1	1	2	3	2	1
*J.Plunkett,A.Manning,D.Pastorini **Lynn Dickey & Ken Anderson ***Joe Thiessmann															
1972	2	1	1				2	2		1	1	1	2*	1	1
													*Brian Sipe		
1973	1*	3**	2***	2	1	2			1	1				5	1
	*Bert Jones **Ron Jaworski ***Dan Fouts					(Ray Guy the punter was also on 1st round)									
1974			3*	3**	1	1		2		1	2	2	3	1	2
			*Danny White	**Mike Boryla											
1975	1*	1			2	2	2**		1		1			3	2
	*Steve Bartkowski						**Pat Haden								
1976	1	2		3	1	1	2	1	1	2	2	2	3		1
			undrafted - Jim Zorn												
1977	2*	1		1	4	2		2	2	3**					
	*Tommy Kramer									**Steve DeBerg					
1978	1*	2	2	2	1	1			2	1	1	1**			
	*Doug Williams			undrafted - Warren Moon & Guido Merkens								**Bill Kenney			

QUARTERBACKS DRAFTED

YEAR	1st	2nd	3rd	4th	5th	6th	7th	8th	9th	10th	11th	12th	13th	14th	15th
1979	3*		1**	1	3	1			2	1	2	1			
1980	2	1		4	1	1	1	3	2			3			
1981	2	1*	1	3				3**	1	2	3	3			
1982	2*	2**		1		2		1	2	1	3	1			
1983	6*				1	2		1	2	2	1	3			
1984		1	3**		2	4	1	1	1	2	2	1			
1985	1*	1**	1			3***			2	2	2****				
1986	2*	1	3	1		1**	1		1	1	2	3			
1987	4*		1	3**			2	1	1	2***	2	3			
1988			2*			3	2		2	2	3	2			
1989	3*	2	2	2		2	2	1		1	1	2			
1990	2*		3**	3	1	2		1	2	1	1	5			

1979: *Phil Simms **Joe Montana

1980: undrafted - Dave Krieg

1981: *Neil Lomax **Wade Wilson

1982: *Jim McMahon **Oliver Luck

1983: *John Elway, Jim Kelly, Dan Marino & Ken O'Brien

1984: *Boomer Esiason **Jeff Hostetler, Jay Schroeder — undrafted - Bill Bates (retired to coach at Nease High School who, under Tim Tebow, won the State Championship)

1985: *Bernie Kosar **Randall Cunningham ***Steve Bono ****Doug Flutie

1986: *Jim Everett **Mark Rypien

1987: *V. Testaverde; C. Miller; Jim Harbaugh **Rich Gannon, Steve Beuerlein ***Don Majkowski

1988: *Tom Tupa & Chris Chandler

1989: *Troy Aikman, Barry Sanders, Derrick Thomas & Deion Sanders

1990: *Jeff George **Neil O'Donnell

QUARTERBACKS DRAFTED

YEAR	1st	2nd	3rd	4th	5th	6th	7th	8th	9th	10th	11th	12th	13th	14th	15th
1991		2*	2	3	1		1			1	1	2			
1992	3	2		3		1*		4	3**	1	1	3			
1993	2*		1		1**		1	3***							
1994	2*			2		1	4**								
1995	2*	2**	undrafted - Kurt Warner & Jeff Garcia	4	1	2	1								
1996			1	1	2	2	2								
1997	1	1*	*Jake Plummer	undrafted - Jake Delhomme	2	2	5								
1998	2*	1	2**	2		2***	1								
1999	5*	1	1	2	1		3								
2000	1	2			1	5*	3								
2001	1*	3**		3	2	2									
2002	3*		1	2**	4	2	4								

*Brett Favre (1991, 2nd)
*Jeff Blake, **Brad Johnson (1992)
*Drew Bledsoe, **Mark Brunell, ***Elvis Grbak & Trent Green (1993)
*Trent Dilfer, **Gus Frerotte (1994); undrafted - Kurt Warner & Jeff Garcia
*S. McNair, K Collins **Kordell Stewart (1995)
undrafted - Jon Kitna (1996)
*Jake Plummer; undrafted - Jake Delhomme (1997)
*Peyton, Ryan Leaf **Brian Griese ***Matt Hasselbeck (1998)
*Donovan McNabb & Daunte Culpepper (1999)
Rd 1: LaVar Arrington & Chris Samuels; *Marc Bulger & Tom Brady (2000)
*Michael Vick **Drew Brees (2001)
*Patrick Ramsey **David Garrard (2002)

QUARTERBACKS DRAFTED

YEAR	1st	2nd	3rd	4th	5th	6th	7th
2003	4*	2	2	1	1	3	2
	*Carson Palmer		undrafted - Tony Romo				
2004	4*		1**	1	1	4	6
	*E.Manning,P.Rivers,B.Roethlisberger **Matt Schaub						
2005	3*		3**	2	2	1***	3*****
	*Alex Smith; Aaron Rodgers **Jason Campbell ***Derek Anderson ****Matt Cassel						
2006	3*	2	2	1	2	2	1
	*Vince Young; Jay Cutler						
2007	2*	3**	1		2	1	1
	*Brady Quinn **Kevin Kolb						
2008	2*	2**	1		4	2***	2
	*M.Ryan,J.Flacco **Chad Henne ***Colt Brennan						
2009	3*	1		1	2	4	
	*Matthew Stafford, Mark Sanchez & Josh Freeman						
2010	2*	1	1**	1	2	4	3
	*S.Bradford,T.Tebow,N.Suh **Colt McCoy						
2011	4*	2**	1		3	1	1
	*Cam Newton **Andy Dalton						
2012	4*	1	2**	1***		1	2
	*A.Luck & RG III **R.Wilson & N.Foles ***Kirk Cousins						
2013	1	1*	1	4**			4
	*Geno Smith **Matt Barkley						
2014	3*	2		2	2	5	
	*Johnny Manziel & Teddy Bridgewater						
2015	2*	2	1	1	1		1
	*Jameis Winston & Marcus Mariota						

www.ingramcontent.com/pod-product-compliance
Lightning Source LLC
LaVergne TN
LVHW010211221225
828287LV00008B/552